Everything New

and WHO'S WHO *in*

CLOWN MINISTRY

With 75 Skits For Special Days

BY
JANET LITHERLAND

MERIWETHER PUBLISHING LTD.
Colorado Springs, Colorado

Meriwether Publishing Ltd., Publisher
Box 7710
Colorado Springs, CO 80933

Editors: Arthur L. Zapel & Rhonda Wray
Typesetting: Sharon E. Garlock
Cover design: Tom Myers
Clown on cover: Trina Hardy

© Copyright MCMXCIII Meriwether Publishing Ltd.
Printed in the United States of America
First Edition

Library of Congress Cataloging-in-Publication Data

Litherland, Janet.
    Everything new and who's who in clown ministry : with 75 skits for special days / by Janet Litherland.
        p.   cm.
    Includes bibliographical references and index.
    ISBN 0-916260-99-2 : $10.95
    1. Clowns--Religious aspects--Christianity. 2. Clowns--Biography.
I. Title.
    BV4235.C47L574   1993
    246'.7--dc20   93-14652
                                                                                   CIP

Scripture marked (NIV) is taken from the HOLY BIBLE, NEW INTERNA-TIONAL VERSION®. Copyright © 1973, 1978, 1984 by International Bible Society. Used by permission of Zondervan Publishing House. All rights reserved.

The "NIV" and "New International Version" trademarks are registered in the United States Patent and Trademark Office by International Bible Society. Use of either trademark requires the permission of International Bible Society.

Scripture marked (KJV) is taken from the King James Version.

Performance Rights

Photographs

The photographs included in this book were provided to the publisher by the featured clowns for use in their profile descriptions. Where the photographer is known a photo credit is given beside the photo. Identification of other photographers will be provided by the featured clowns.

TABLE OF CONTENTS

PREFACE

Clowns who are in ministry are in the business of touching souls. It's funny business, but it's also serious business, because it defines the Christian life — both for the clown and for those to whom he or she ministers. These clowns are called "clown ministers," "ministry clowns," "church clowns," and "gospel clowns." The terms are interchangeable. To reserve the title "clown minister" only for ordained ministers who clown is to nitpick. All who are called to follow Christ are also called to minister in his name.

Though clown ministry has been around for centuries, the form as we know it is a relatively new phenomenon, little more than two decades old. It was pioneered by Floyd Shaffer ("Socataco"), a Lutheran pastor who saw it as "a personal Christian journey, a journey into servanthood and childlikeness." Others gradually picked up the idea, affording it a slow, steady growth until the early 1980s, when it suddenly exploded like popcorn across America. Some clown ministers were very good and some were very bad. Some entertained and forgot to minister, and some ministered and forgot to entertain. The good ones tickled funny bones and touched souls.

In 1982 I wrote *The Clown Ministry Handbook*, the first complete text on this unique form of service. I tracked it to its biblical beginnings and reported on its evolution through the centuries, including its updated version, its intent, and its surge of growth. Now, more than a decade later, clown ministry is taking hold of its big feet and planting them on firm ground. The clown ministers who have lasted wear scars of experience. They are living examples of what worked and what didn't.

Three of the clown ministers in this book appeared in *The Clown Ministry Handbook* in 1982. We're checking in with them again to see what progress they've made, both in their clowning and in their ministry. The others have been carefully selected from across America and around the world — clown ministers whose enduring (and endearing!) work is making a difference in people's lives. They share their experience, failures, successes, and tips to provide inspiration to clown minis-

1

ters everywhere; and they share some of their proven skits and routines simply to spread the blessings. The loving, giving nature of these people is deeply appreciated by the author of this book, for it is only through unselfish sharing that this unique ministry will continue to expand.

This book concentrates on professionalism — improving the performance level of clown ministry for those who already have a grip on the basics. Beginning clown ministers who are looking for the "where and how" of clown ministry, costume and make-up techniques, organizing groups, a theology of clowning, and the development of a clown person need to consult the latest edition of *The Clown Ministry Handbook*.

J. L.

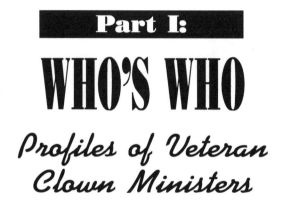

Part I:
WHO'S WHO
Profiles of Veteran Clown Ministers

CHAPTER ONE

CLOWNS OF GOD

Where They Were — Where They Are —
Where They're Going

When *The Clown Ministry Handbook* was first published in 1982, the editor wrote, "We venture to publish this first book on clown ministry because we believe that this activity will grow into another valuable expression of Christian celebration and outreach." In more than a decade since, clown ministry has certainly done that. Thousands of clowns of all shapes, sizes, ages, and abilities are now channeling their creative energy and humor into Christian ministry all over the world. They work alone, or in pairs, or in groups, dusting off denominational differences and leaping over language barriers. The clowns, who are "new creatures," are truly "going into all the world and preaching the gospel" to ordinary mortals, wherever they encounter them.

Some clowns never talk, some talk faster and louder than magpies. Some are liturgical, some are evangelical. Some are whimsical, free spirits who float comfortably between both worlds. Some work only in places suited to outreach ministry, such as hospitals, schools, prisons, and retirement villages; others work in secular settings, such as carnivals, civic events, and street corners; and still others work right smack in the middle of worship services. It's a fact: Wherever they are, these lovable creatures can be outrageously effective. People watch, people listen, and people respond. Only a pillar of stone could miss the message that flows from the heart of a truly dedicated clown minister.

There have been changes in the last decade. Notable is the increasing use of professional-looking costumes, sophisticated equipment, well-designed materials, and continuing education. And why not? We live in a progressive society, where instant information and mind-boggling technology are the norm. Daily, we are exposed to computers, copiers, tapes, television, jet planes, microwaves, fax machines, detailed lesson plans, and step-by-step instructions. Most churches are keeping pace, but some lag behind. For young people of today, lagging ministries — even lagging *clown* ministries — seem hopelessly out-of-date. It's true that the beauty of clown ministry is in its simplicity — that's still there. But simplicity is now the result of careful, practiced calculation rather than makeshift happenstance. Today's clown ministers are picking up the enlightened ball and bouncing it — delivering the old-fashioned message in new-fashioned, funny ways.

Promotional Materials

The Salvation Army's Ebel family ("Kids-Celebration Circus," see page 14) has an interesting package of promotional materials that includes posters, bulletin inserts, a clown coloring contest ("You must be present to win"), and booklets on such subjects as "Leading a Child to Christ" and "Making Little People Feel Big." Especially interesting is the "Salvation Army Corps Kit," which is sent ahead to help congregations prepare for the family's arrival. It includes instructions for recruiting a "staff" of registrars, captains, altar workers, and refreshment servers, and gives detailed information on their duties, beginning two weeks in advance. (The Ebels maintain an exhausting yet rewarding schedule, performing a 1½- to 2-hour show 5 days a week at one location.) The kit also promotes availability for "Laugh and Learn" school assemblies on current topics, such as drugs, peer pressure, and stranger-proofing children.

Expanded Subject Areas

It is interesting to note that the above topics are no longer taboo in clown ministry. J. T. Sikes, whose story appears on page 17, teaches a clown class on substance abuse. "As a Christian in today's world," he says, "you have to know that drugs are destroying families." His class shows how to use standard props, magic tricks, puppets, and storytelling to get the anti-drug message out. He also incorporates a "Say No to Drugs" routine (page 246) into all of his performing events.

David W. Lloyd and his group (page 27) also deal with strong subjects, many of which are chosen for them by their church's worship committee, including feminism, pregnancy, weaponry, the homeless, and "Lent — Journeying into the Darkness of the Unknown."

Education and Training

Education and training for clown ministers is now the expected way to go. No longer are novices putting on Mom's make-up and attic rags and venturing out unprepared, only to wander around and wave. Janet Tucker, a clown for 14 years (page 33), says, "For years, it was common practice for church clowns to say 'I only do clown ministry, so I don't need clown shoes or a wig or entertainment skills.' I believe that a good gospel clown must first be a good clown, and that make-up, costume, and entertainment skills should be of the highest quality to serve the Lord." Roly Bain of England (page 52) concurs: "It's too easy just to have clowns doing drama, as if the clown garb is simply another costume. Clowns need to be well rehearsed as well as well presented to be as professional as they can be — really good and properly foolish!" Clown ministers like Janet and Roly, who have been serving for years, believe this so strongly that they take regular refresher courses for themselves. They're keeping current.

Carolyn Costley (page 21), who trains other clowns, still takes extensive training every year to improve her own clown person. The Ebenezer Troupe of Clowns (page 24) holds regular workshops for their members and prospects, and offers an extended "graduation" experience to ensure that their clowns are prepared. Trudy Cravatta-DiNardo (page 35) stretched her skills by taking a course in sign language — an excellent idea for clown ministers!

Still another means of continuing education, or keeping current, comes to us from Philip Noble of Scotland (page 49). He derives the most help, and by far the most encouragement, from staying in close touch with other clowns through correspondence, especially "tape letters" — videos.

Regarding television as a means of getting the message out to the public, Philip has discovered drawbacks. He says, "My experience with television has not been totally positive. In the past I have done some pieces but now feel reluctant to

7

do so. The clown (especially a 'Reverend' clown) has immediate curiosity and novelty value for the masses, but I miss the audience reaction and participation. Also, material that may have taken years to perfect can, in ten minutes' exposure on national television, be unusable in the future." . . . Something to think about.

Information Service

The old saying, "Everyone loves a clown," is not necessarily true. For that reason, Kay Turner (see page 40) believes in informing the congregation *and clergy* about the purpose of clowns in church and their many areas of service. "Worship is very personal for some people," Kay says. "A clown can seem intrusive. Children may be frightened, adults annoyed, and the clergy may not accept the art of clowning as appropriate for worship."

Don't assume your pastor understands clown ministry. Learn from Kay's experience: "When I first began clowning, I felt blessed and wanted to share my new art form with the church. I met with a few others who were interested in clowning, and we began learning together. We felt accepted by the church and knew of no conflicts. Then we asked to perform a skit in worship. After the pastor watched our rehearsal, he said 'No.' He didn't care for the silent performance, because 'someone in the congregation may not understand.' When asked if *he* understood, he said 'Yes,' and gave an accurate account of the skit's intent. Though he never said, we eventually realized that to him, clowns were acceptable for social gatherings but not worship. No matter how we tried over the next two years, we were not allowed to participate as worship clowns. It didn't seem to be a problem with the congregation, only with the pastor." Kay takes some of the blame herself. "We should have met with him at the very beginning," she says, "to discuss our intentions and hear his opinions. A lot of time and feelings could have been saved to be used in a more meaningful way." Clowns are learning to move slowly and purposefully with congregations and clergy to build strong, lasting ministries.

8

And yet another kind of information: Tim Morrison (see page 68) asks some pointed questions about clown ministers, like himself, who are between "run of the mill" and professional, whose busy lives allow only a minimum of clowning time. We suspect that most of the clowns out there fit into this category, and several have been included in this book. We also suspect that many, by nature of the clown, are more prone to discuss only the "up sides," painting a much brighter picture than actually exists. For this reason, the clowns in this book were asked to share some bad experiences, failures, or mistakes, so that others might benefit. They have provided good information. Clown ministers, rather than being secretive and possessive of their experiences and material — which was often the case in the past — are now openly sharing with one another to promote the *work*. Okay, so they may hold back a "secret ingredient" or two, but doesn't every good cook?

Professional Organizations

Support groups have become more important to clown ministers in the last decade, organizations such as the World Clown Association, Clowns of America International, Phoenix Power & Light Company, Inc., the Fellowship of Christian Magicians, and local Clown Alleys. These groups and others like them pursue excellence in clowning, whether sacred or secular, and offer workshops to achieve that purpose. They also hold conventions, where clowns can meet one another, share experiences, and find inspiration. Randy Christensen (page 30), who has served as Clown Ministry Chairman for the World Clown Association, finds these opportunities invaluable. He says, "I have come to know and love clowns from around the world who have taught me and inspired me. This is crucial."

Hospital Ministry

Another change is in hospital ministry. Hospitals are much more open to clowns than they were a decade ago. There is an enormous need for this ministry, but in the past clowns were more of a hindrance than a help. St. James Hospital in Chicago Heights, Illinois, has a "Humor and Therapy Department" where clowns, including Janet Tucker (mentioned previously), visit each Wednesday. Kathleen Deegan (page 24) was a resident chaplain at Grady Memorial Hospital in Atlanta, Georgia, and often made her rounds as "Gracie the Clown." "The staff was always hugging me as Gracie," she says. "They made me promise to come back!"

Forward-thinking clown ministers have become more businesslike in their approach to hospitals; more willing to plan their visits and to abide by the rules. J. T. Sikes (the clown trainer mentioned previously) specializes in clowning for the ill. In his classes on hospital clowning, he teaches how to get started, whom to contact, what questions to ask, what to do or not to do, what can and cannot be said to patients. Instruction covers restricted areas, waiting room clowning, and proper giveaways. The "informed approach" is the new trend — and it's working!

For a special kind of hospital ministry, see the story of Jim and June Gorgans on page 38. They serve in disaster areas and relief centers. And for a very different perspective on nursing home ministry ("It's not for everyone!"), meet Kay Turner, whose wonderfully wise words rise from the blessings of her own inner healing (page 40).

Extended Outreach

For a long time, ministry clowns ministered only in church settings — Sunday school, Bible school, fellowship meetings, church suppers. Then they started reaching out — prisons, hospitals, nursing homes, centers for the developmentally disabled — places where they were welcomed and loved, but where they were expected to "be religious." Clown ministers, however, do not necessarily do anything religious; but a religious message can usually be gleaned from things they do. They function first as clowns, second as ministers. It is this thought that has opened up new territory in the last ten years. It is no longer "wrong" for ministry clowns to venture out of the church. Many are now going beyond the bounds of the sacred and into the realm of opportunity. Oddly, (or is it providential?) this secular realm is providing a means for the clown minister to be at his or her sacred best.

Kay Turner and Philip Noble (both mentioned above) believe in the validity of extended outreach. In addition to her church clowning, Kay works at civic events, campgrounds, country clubs, libraries, and even does promotions for businesses. Philip, who is an Episcopalian rector, reaches beyond his church to festivals, street corners, and theaters. He says, "I see my clown most effective as part of an outreach event for those not readily open to the written Word." Dennis Clare (page 63) has gone with musicians into hotels, a common meeting place for the rock generation in his native Australia. It works, because the audience is surprised (and pleased!) by the presence of a clown in this kind of situation.

Tommy Thomson of Scotland (see page 65) says, "I will go anywhere, try anything once — I even did a spot at a charity disco for a Bible group — but I trust God that his will will be done, whatever I am invited to do."

CHAPTER TWO

CLOWNS ACROSS AMERICA

With clown ministers and ministries in America now numbering into the thousands, choosing which to profile was not an easy task. (Clowns from Puerto Rico, an American territory, are profiled in Chapter 3, *Clowns Around the World,* because their native language is Spanish and their perspective is distinctly and marvelously different!)

Each person selected for this book has something unique to share about his or her ministry — something that will benefit other clown ministers, whatever their level of experience. Presented here are individuals, partners, couples, families, and troupes. Some represent the liturgical perspective, some the evangelical. Some are extremely conservative, some are liberal to the other extreme. But *all* are successfully involved in spreading the Word of God. . . Repeat, *successfully.*

This is an opportunity to learn and to grow.

Photo by Tony Jagnesak

Left: KIDS-CELEBRATION CIR-CUS: P-Nut, Happy-Go-Litely, Baby Ruth Bipper, Lazy Daisy

Right: The Ebel Family: Auxiliary Captains David and Diane, Josh, Ruth Ann, Jesse Daniel

KIDS-CELEBRATION CIRCUS

Meet the Salvation Army's first full-time clown ministry family, the Ebels: Auxiliary Captains David "Happy-Go-Litely," and Diane "Lazy Daisy," and their children, Josh "P-Nut," Ruth Ann "Baby Ruth," and Jesse Daniel "Bipper." They are Divisional Evangelists, serving northern California and Nevada.

When this family appeared in 1982's *The Clown Ministry Handbook*, the ministry was chiefly David's, with occasional appearances by Diane and the children. At that time David was State Evangelist for the Church of God in Georgia and, on the side, the family was just beginning their own "Love Family Ministries," an outreach program of evangelism, Bible study, children's church, Sunday school, and neighborhood gatherings. As the children grew, so did the ministry, and one by one, the family followed David into clowning.

The Ebels are evangelicals. Presentations are fast-paced, energy-packed segments that blend into a full service, which always ends at the altar. "The altar is the most important part," David says. "In each performance, the love and forgiveness of Jesus Christ is presented on a childlike level so that people of all ages can make a decision to accept Jesus Christ as Lord and Savior."

Their flexible format goes something like this:

Theme Music (fanfare, background)

Welcome

Fun Songs (audience participation)

Skit

Illusions

Puppets } Choose one or more, interwoven with jug-

Storytelling   gling, ballooning, and

Ventriloquism   other skills.

Altar

At the altar, David offers the choices of the night — sin or Jesus, explaining that "Giants" (sins) are what separate us from the love of God, and that it is his good pleasure to forgive us our sins.

Results show that this kind of ministry works for them. From the official records of the Church of God, David's personal statistics from October, 1977, to September, 1992 (His Church of God credentials were surrendered after he had served with the Salvation Army for six months): 17,888 saved, 721 reclaimed, 245 baptized, and 3,037 sermons preached.

David entered clowning through the back door — literally. As a volunteer helping with a "Kids' Krusade" in a local church, he was asked to dress up in a clown suit and play with the children at the close of the service.

"While I stood in the back of the church in my rented costume," he says, "I saw several children peeking in the windows. I stuck my head out and invited them in, but they said their parents wouldn't let them inside our 'crazy people's church.' I responded by presenting the gospel to them through the doorway, then telling them to go home, kneel at the foot of their beds and pray, giving their hearts to Jesus. They ran off, but a little while later there was a knock at the door and children's voices calling, 'Clown!!!' When I stuck my head out the door again, I found eight children with tears in their eyes saying, 'We gave our hearts to Jesus and we know he's real.' At that moment the Holy Spirit spoke to me: 'You keep telling me you would do anything for me . . . Will you love my children?' And that began the clown in my life."

The Ebel family's clown ministry has taken them all over the United States, including Hawaii, and to Jamaica, Bermuda, the Bahamas, and Canada. They have been featured at national conventions of The Fellowship of Christian Magicians, Southeast Clown Association, World Clown Association, Clown Cavalcade, Circus Magic, and the National Clown Arts Council's Clownfest. They were also asked to minister for the Salvation's Army's Territorial Congress.

"Our goal," David says, "is to be a quality resource to every corps and church and an excitement and encouragement to every child."

Kids-Celebration Circus's Tips for Working With Children

1. Never make a child the "butt" of a joke. A joke is only funny when all parties enjoy the comedy.

2. Many children have no idea what a clown really is. Sudden movements that are funny to adults can leave a child trembling with fear.

3. Know when to stay and when to walk away. One child may follow you anywhere; another will enjoy you more from a distance.

4. Discourage pushy parents by enlisting their help: "Hold it right there, Mom. We're scared! Could you back him up a little so he can see me better?"

See also *Meat of the Word?* (Page 249) by David Ebel.

16

Photo by Tony Jagnesak

BUBBA D. CLOWN

J. T. Sikes, "Bubba D. Clown," is a Southern Baptist Louisiana native who is a full-time Naval Officer and part-time professional clown. His motto is: *Normal is Boring!*

"When I perform for a military audience," he says, "I salute the enlisted personnel and address them as 'sir.' Then I walk right past the officers." That's not normal, and it's certainly not boring. He gets a laugh every time. To J. T., laughter is the best medicine. It is especially important in clown ministry, where it is sometimes easy to get wrapped up in pastoring and forget clowning. "Remember," he says, "when you are in make-up, you are a CLOWN, not a pastor. Make your performance funny, exciting, and loving, and the doors for your personal ministry will open."

Doors opened early for J. T., though he didn't realize they were leading to clown ministry. Becoming an Eagle Scout at age 15 and a Cubmaster at age 18 taught him leadership. The U. S. Navy developed his leadership talents, and marriage and children taught him personal responsibility. In the first 14 years of his Naval career, he spent many months away from his family, learning the importance of love and how God strengthens in times of loneliness. During the last 12 years as a Naval Officer, he has had hundreds of opportunities to counsel and help others. He has been stationed from coast to coast and has been to 36 countries. "Each time I move on," he says, "my heart is burdened by friends I must leave behind. This feeling of loss is somehow turned to hope for others when I clown."

While on active duty, he served congregations as Youth Leader, Youth Minister, Single Adult Director, and Deacon. How does all this relate to clown ministry? J. T. says, "I believe that God was grooming me to understand people and their problems, so that I could be an effective clown minister. I know what parents go through, how teenagers feel, the needs of single adults, and after rearing two children, I know about schedule problems!"

"Bubba D. Clown" emerged in an unusual way. In his own words: "I had just returned from a six-month deployment of my unit in Sicily and read about a 10K Walk-a-thon for Multiple Sclerosis. So I asked some of my men if they'd join me in representing our Navy Squadron for this worthy cause. Well, twenty of us had walked about two blocks when a young boy passed us in a wheelchair. He was sweating and struggling, and this really touched my heart. I thought, that's not fair — we're casually walking and that boy is really struggling for his cause. Why not make this meaningful and challenging? I asked one of my men if he'd like to walk the 10K backwards. He agreed and we walked the rest of the course that way. About a block from the finish line a clown approached me and said, 'I've been watching you all morning and you've got to be one of the craziest people I've ever seen. Do you realize that you aren't going to be able to move tomorrow because of sore muscles? You should be a clown.' She was right. I ached miserably the next morning, and I also knew I wanted to be a clown."

"Bubba" isn't just a clown. He's an award-winning clown minister who works everywhere — hospitals, nursing homes, fairs, corporate events, birthday parties, and worship services. He has performed in Iceland for the U. S. Embassy. While there,

18

he established the Glacier Clown Alley at Naval Air Station Keflavik and it is still active.

"In Iceland I learned to perform as a silent clown," he says, "because I didn't speak Icelandic." It worked fine — giving credence to the idea that clowns are universal. He has also performed for ambassadors from foreign countries, and for military audiences through USO Overseas. His awards include Skit Competition, Gospel Clowning, Paradability, and the Betty Lewis Memorial Award, given each year to the person who best displays clowning from the heart.

He is a member of the World Clown Association, Clowns of America International, and is currently Chaplain of the Southeast Clown Association. He is also a Clown Alley trainer, specializing in clowning for the ill. In this regard, he has a solo ministry at Humana Hospital in Orange Park, Florida, where he visits patients, family members, and staff every week. He still remembers his first visit, when an elderly, depressed woman responded to his ministry. She came out of her depression, started recovering, and was released within a week. "Yes," he says, "there is power in love and laughter!"

Bubba's Tips for Hospital and Nursing Home Visits

1. No loud noises.

2. No touching special equipment. (IVs, traction units, monitors)

3. No sitting on beds.

4. No touching covered parts of the body. Under the cover could be a crushed foot, infected leg, or appendages that have had surgery.

5. Never give candy to patients. Always ask permission to give balloons.

6. Keep your visit short.

7. LEARN FROM MY MISTAKE: Never congratulate new parents until first checking with nurses' station to ensure the birth was normal. I once congratulated a young woman only to have her burst into tears because she had just lost

19

her baby. Nothing like putting a size 18 clown shoe in your mouth!

See also *No-Prop Clowning* (page 244), and *Things Aren't Always What They Seem* (page 246) by J. T. Sikes.

Left: Spatz

Right: Carolyn Costley

Spatz, Jr. not pictured

SPATZ AND SPATZ, JR.

Imagine a clown who in her spare time pursues the scholarly study of humor, who is "particularly interested in the effects of different types of humor on cognitive processes and memory." . . . Can someone who thinks like that be FUNNY? You bet!

Meet Carolyn Costley, "Spatz," a university marketing professor in Texas who surprises college students with her clown persona during long days of registering for classes, and uses performance techniques and humor in her classroom.

"Knowing that laughter can help students loosen up and open up," Carolyn says, "I use some laughter-generating exercises early in the semester. It helps everyone get comfortable with each other and with me, reduces stress, and builds a relationship. With that rapport, I feel I can communicate better for the rest of the semester." At the end of the semester she hosts a pie-throwing party for her students! Wouldn't it be great to have Spatz for a professor? Let's sit in on a lesson:

"I believe that education makes us better clowns, and

21

that clown ministers should be guided by rules, as are secular clowns. It is very important to me that the clowns whom I train or work with be knowledgeable about clown etiquette, the historical basis of clown ministry, make-up, and character traditions. While 'rules are made to be broken,' it is important to first understand the intent of those rules in order to maintain their integrity when deviating from tradition. Clowning around can and should be fun. To be 'real' clowns, however, we should treat clowning as serious business.

"I have found that a few words from the pulpit (education) about clowns' historical role in the church can ease anxiety and negative reactions. Pastors with advanced or broad education tend to be more accepting, even proactive, about clowns in worship. One such pastor even *suggested* that I ride a bicycle down the center aisle to illustrate how Jesus might enter a town on Palm Sunday today. In many groups this would be outrageously sacrilegious, but this was for the children's sermon, which is a 'safe' place for a clown to show up. Now I try to educate congregations by speaking to Sunday school classes and other church groups, conducting clown workshops, and making appearances on 'safe' occasions, such as Rally Day and Shrove Tuesday." (Note: Spatz is so well respected that her picture is in the church directory!)

Contrary to popular belief, all children do not love clowns. Most clown ministers have stories to relate about children's fear of them or even hostility toward them. Carolyn handled one such situation this way: "More than once I've found that education helps alleviate children's fear of me as a clown. For my special friends Jeremy and Patrick, I did personal demonstrations of make-up application. Neither of them wanted to be made up, but watching me make the transition to clown helped ease their discomfort. Jeremy played invisible ball with me after that. Before the demonstration, he couldn't stand to be in the same room with me."

Carolyn believes in continuing education for herself, too. Every year she trains with Phoenix Performing Arts Ministries, of which she is a member of the Board of Directors. During the year she attends training sessions sponsored by the

University of Wisconsin — LaCrosse Clown Camp on the Road.

As Spatz or Spatz, Jr. (a younger version of Spatz), Carolyn does mainly improvisational clowning — meet-and-greet, one-on-one interactions — at picnics, festivals, parades, malls, hospitals, and in worship settings. Her encounters are usually brief and intended to make people feel special — things like dusting the sidewalk, or opening visible and invisible doors.

She also interprets Scripture. "I'm serious about my humor," she says.

Spatz's Tips Learned From Children

1. Clowns don't have pierced ears. (Not much she can do about that.)

2. Clowns don't have long fingernails. (She cut them.)

3. "Three Cheers for the Holiday" walkarounds with boxes of Cheer detergent aren't funny.

4. Playing invisible ball *is* funny.

See also *Looking for God in All the Wrong Places* (page 239), and *The Gift* (page 172) by Carolyn Costley.

Kathleen "Gracie" Deegan and Gracie

Gracie and friends from E.T.C.: Amy Miller, Jennifer Evans, Molly Wallace, Jessica Livingston, Chris Brown, Erin Akin.

GRACIE AND E. T. C.
(Kathleen Deegan & the Ebenezer Troupe of Clowns)

Here is a brand-new troupe of clowns that bears watching. Under the direction of the Reverend Kathleen Deegan, "Gracie," a United Methodist minister, they've been to school, passed the exams, graduated, and gone to work. This is a 23-member, multi-age troupe of older children, youth, and adults, including a complete family — Mom, Dad, and three girls. Kathleen likes the idea of mixed ages. She says, "Teenagers are great at day care centers; children are fantastic at nursing homes; adults are wonderful everywhere and, of course, they're our built-in drivers and chaperons!"

Ebenezer Troupe of Clowns (Conyers, Georgia), called E. T. C., has a six-week training program that concentrates on development of the clown and sharing of the Christian witness in places like a Cub Scout celebration, the Special Olympics, and fundraising events. Their graduation is an event in itself, spread over 11 days! New groups take note:

"Our 'graduation plunge' begins immediately after Sunday morning service. We put on our make-up and costumes and head for the local nursing home, our first outing together. We learned that within 15 minutes our newest clowns will use up all their ticklers, and they'll still have 45 minutes left! That's when I see the transformation — that's when they begin to share themselves," says Kathleen. "They slow down, listen to people, hug, and do spontaneous skits. Some of our teenagers sing hymns with folks while children will simply dance with joy! They become true Clowns for Christ as they let go and share themselves.

"Then we go back to the church for our 'formal' graduation — diplomas, cake, punch, and plenty of guests who have come to help us celebrate. The next Sunday we do the entire worship service, and the following Wednesday night we do skits and face painting and give out balloons."

The great thing about this extended graduation is that it offers the troupe immediate experience in a variety of situations where they're all together, giving one another love and support. It cuts way down on first-time jitters. Graduation also makes the troupe feel special, particularly when members of the congregation are there to cheer them on. The troupe now publishes the *E. T. C. Newsletter* to keep folks informed about what's going on in their collective lives and ministry.

E. T. C.'s inspiration, "Gracie," was born during Kathleen's seminary years at Emory University in Atlanta, Georgia. "I wanted to put on grease paint and my hat every chance I could, so I'd invent places to go," she says. But when she visited the children at Grady Memorial Hospital, she realized she was hooked on clown ministry. She became resident chaplain of Grady's Clinical Pastoral Education program and often made her rounds as "Gracie." Later, when she became the Associate Minister at Ebenezer, she found that Gracie was lonely and wanted friends — and that's when E. T. C. was born.

Now, Kathleen is Minister of Program at First United Methodist Church in Elberton, Georgia, where Gracie has a new mission; and Pam Akin "Nellie," and Tina Marshburn "Dottie," are leading E. T. C.

Gracie's Tips for Clown Groups

1. Don't stand around and be cute — do something!
2. Adapt skits to suit your situation.
3. Develop individual clown "specialties."
4. Commit to being IN MINISTRY — IN-VOLVED! (That way you won't lose sight of your purpose, which is sharing the Christian witness.)

See also *Perfect 10* (page 209), by Kathleen Deegan, and *Free Love* (page 108) by Pam Akin for Gracie and E. T. C.

From left to right: Cop a Plea, Poppatui and David W. Lloyd.

COP A PLEA & POPPATUI
(David W. Lloyd and the Faith and Fantasy Group of the Seekers Faith Community of the Church of the Saviour)

Here is a Washington, D. C., clown group quite a bit different from E. T. C. (immediately preceding pages) and a whole lot different from the evangelical Kids-Celebration Circus (page 14). Their congregation is distinctly liberal and insists on political correctness. They use an inclusive language lectionary and always balance the gender of whomever is preaching with the opposing gender to be liturgist.

One of the tenets of the Church of the Saviour is to honor all the divergent beliefs and practices within the Roman Catholic, Protestant, and Orthodox traditions, and the church's worship committee chooses themes for the clown group. Themes are heavy, psychological, and can be very tough: Advent as pregnancy, Lent as living into the darkness of our spirits.

Leader of the clown group, David W. Lloyd ("Cop a Plea" and "Poppatui"), says, "Most of the clowns are a little more theologically conservative, though a bit off-center, and in any case are predisposed to poke fun at sacred cows." This attitude

27

comes out in their skits. (Check out their "off-center" skits in Chapters 4 and 5.)

David is an attorney who, when choosing his clown person, needed to deal with his role as an authority figure. So he decided to be a Keystone Kop. "I'll never forget," he says, "the excitement of finding a clown name. While reading Paul's letter to the Romans, I saw the passage about Jesus being our advocate rather than our accuser. I said to myself, "I'd just have to cop a plea . . . Cop a Plea. That's it! That's my clown name — Cop a Plea!" Several years later, when he had to get in touch with his "needy side," he tried being a tramp clown, and "Poppatui" was born. "It was wonderful! While my Keystone Kop will talk if need be, 'Poppatui' is always silent."

David was involved with the National Clown, Mime, Puppetry, Dance, and Storytelling Workshops during the early 1980s, assisting the director and teaching classes in characterization and script development. He was part of the group that created Phoenix Power and Light and was a member of their Board of Directors for several years. He now serves as their legal consultant. As a clown minister, he's been around a long time and has stumbled into, and climbed out of, most of the potholes that await new clowns. Experienced clowns, too, can learn a great deal from the unique flavor of his ministry.

David, along with Marjory and Peter Bankson, Randi and Skip Banks, Doug Dodge, Alan Dragoo, Ellen Griffith, Mollie McMurray, and Cindy Timmerman Pedder comprise the current Faith and Fantasy group. This group started in 1977 in response to a clown worship service put on by one of Floyd Shaffer's groups. They met weekly for several years, then bi-weekly, clowning in hospitals and nursing homes, as well as in worship services. They also began teaching workshops, and out of those experiences David and Peter developed a 12-week clown ministry curriculum, *Faith and Fantasy, An Introduction to Christian Clowning.* It is a comprehensive course that blends prayer, technical input, activity, practice, individual reflection, and group sharing. It also requires commitment. Clowns who take their course take it seriously (but not solemnly!).

During the last few years, they have decreased consider-
ably their number of performance and teaching outings. Why?
"We're older, busier (David is also the current director of The
National Center on Child Abuse and Neglect), and more tired,"
says David. "But I also think that American society is more
serious and intolerant, less willing to play than it was in the
1960s and 70s." . . . Could this be true? . . . Is this something
clown ministers need to work on?

Cop a Plea's Tips for Advanced Clowning

1. Distinct clown personalities and appropriate names have
   been important to our group. We have watched our characters develop and even change over the years. After we'd
   known one another for several years and felt comfortable
   with our characters, we tried an exercise that promoted
   change. We each allowed another person to apply our clown
   make-up for us as that person saw and understood our clown.
   It worked well for us, but we believe it takes a certain
   amount of trust and a willingness to be vulnerable to be
   able to do this, and we do not recommend it for novice clowns.

2. We have found that spontaneously picking out one or more
   people from the congregation to be involved in skits works
   well. In our Nativity Play (page 222), for example, all
   characters except Mary, Joseph, and Herod were chosen
   from the congregation and costumes quickly put on them.

3. To avert disaster, we "back up" all props with mime versions
   of same. Don't depend too heavily on trick props.

4. We do not leave messes behind. We pick up our props and
   trash. *We also pick up messy situations by processing them
   with those affected.*

See also *The Summons* (page 143) and *The 20th Century
Mystery Play* (page 222) by David W. Lloyd and the Faith and
Fantasy Group of the Seekers Faith Community of the Church
of the Saviour, and *The Hat Shop* (page 137), by Alan Dragoo
and Ellen Griffith, submitted by David W. Lloyd.

Left: Micah the Clown; upper: Simon de Clown; lower: Randy Christenson with Ben.

SIMON DE CLOWN AND MICAH THE CLOWN

These two clowns belong to one person, the Reverend Randy Christensen, a children's pastor in Milwaukee, Wisconsin. Simon is a Tramp clown, Micah a Whiteface. All three of these people appeared in the original *The Clown Ministry Handbook*.

Randy's clown ministry has always been with children, because it was in a children's hospital, dressed up as a one-time-only clown that he found his clown-calling. A friend had insisted, "If you'll try clowning just once, I'll never ask you again." So he dressed up and grudgingly went his "one time."

"Each room I stepped into brought a new sense of ministry," Randy says. "Broken children's expressions lit up, eyes twinkled and laughter echoed. Before we left, we went into the Intensive Care Unit. A tiny girl was sitting up with tubes running in and out of her. Her mother and a nurse stood nearby. I didn't know what to do, so I juggled. (Not a great idea in ICU, but I wasn't prepared with options.) I only stayed a couple of minutes, but when I left — I'll never forget these words — the little girl's mother said, 'Look! She's trying to blow kisses to

30

you!' I stepped into the hall and was overwhelmed. It was then I prayed and the Lord gave me the burden for children."

When we checked in with Randy ten years ago, he was already an experienced clown minister (as both "Simon" and "Micah") and a children's pastor. During the last decade, his techniques have expanded to include puppetry, ventriloquism, illusions, cartooning, music, and storytelling. He is another of those clown ministers who pursues excellence in clowning. He says, "I have spoken with ministry clowns who say, 'I don't want to look too good as a clown because it may draw attention to me rather than to the message.' Their reasoning is erroneous," he continues. "Clown make-up, whether it looks professional or not, draws attention to the wearer! So why not give our best to the Lord? Please realize, God wants humble successes, not humble failures." To support this, Randy cites Psalms 33:3 ("play skillfully") and II Corinthians 13:11 ("aim for perfection"). "God has challenged me to commit to excellence in clowning," he says, "but even more than that, to commit myself to growing into the man of God that he desires me to be. If each of us will do that, the world will be changed for his glory."

Vaudeville and the silent movie era have influenced Randy's clowning. He believes that many of the "tried and true" formulas for comedy are performed by these old masters. "Besides," he says, "it's been fun to sit with my own children and laugh at Charlie Chaplin and Buster Keaton time after time."

Which brings us to the final major influence on Randy's clowning — his own children. From their continued sense of wonder at the commonplace, to his five-year-old's beating on his chest like Tarzan ("I'm just mixing up my food, Dad!"), Randy is getting a close-up view of the world through the eyes of children. That is what truly great clowns must learn to do.

Randy Christensen has served as Clown Ministry Chairman for the World Clown Association and as the Clown Department Chairman of the Fellowship of Christian Magicians. He has taught at their conventions and written for their publications. In 1991 he taught and performed at the World Clown Convention in England. There, he was enchanted by the whimsical world of European clowning. (Meet some of these wonderfully different kinds of clown ministers in Chapter 3, *Clowns Around the World* (page 47). "But even more crucial," Randy says, "I have come to know and love clowns from around the world who have taught me and inspired me." Some of Randy's "inspirations," both at home and abroad, are profiled elsewhere in this book.

Simon's and Micah's Very Best Tip

Skits allow you the opportunity to show your audience how your clown thinks, feels, and reacts. So, develop your clown *character*. Let your unique sense of humor, reasoning process, and emotional response shine through.

Randy closes with a funny experience: "One Sunday morning, while on the way to a church service in full make-up and costume, I was stopped by a police officer. What a surprise when he 'frisked' me! And can you imagine the look on the small child's face as he rode by in another car? Since I was an 'out-of-stater,' the officer debated whether I needed to be taken down to the station. Thank God he decided that was not necessary!"

Will some clever clown minister develop this experience into a skit . . . and let his or her *character* shine through?

See also *Testimony Food* (page 234) by Randy Christensen.

JELLY BEAN

A minister has several different functions — teacher, preacher, administrator, one-on-one shareperson, prayerperson, and businessperson. Janet "Jelly Bean" Tucker believes that a clown minister has the same areas of opportunity but is able to take them one step further by putting the "clown" into them. She sees the clown as a unique interpreter of concepts and ideas concerning God's word: "Following a clown ministry program, those watching will often say, 'I never thought about it that way before.' "

"It's the comic character that enables all to understand," Janet says, and the *all* is significant. "Children react to the clown as a character who is simply funny and cheerful; older children begin to see the story or parable the clown is performing; and more mature Christians see the deeper meanings of a true Christian lifestyle of love in the clown's antics."

Beginning clown ministers entertain, inspire, and share, but as they become more accomplished, they discover more and more opportunities to be of service. Because they are awarded these opportunities that others never have, Janet Tucker wants these clowns to be the best they can be. "Jelly Bean" was a secular clown — parties, stage shows, promotions — before becoming a clown minister, and her goal has always been to upgrade the quality of clowns doing gospel clowning. "Knowing how to be a proper clown — good make-up, professional-looking costume, and quality skills should come first for the gospel clown, before he or she tries to perform skits or presentations," she says. "Clown ministers must be traditional, funny, exciting, and *excellent* in both their clowning and their ministry."

Janet's excellence shows in her many credits: In 1987 she was appointed as the first Clown Ministry Director of the World Clown Association. In 1991 she became president of that organization during their historic convention in Bognor Regis, England. She lives in Indiana and is Instructor of Clown Arts at Purdue University. She also lectures annually at conventions for the Fellowship of Christian Magicians, and in 1990 was a delegate to the International Clown Summit in Dalkeith, Scotland.

Janet is an excellent skit-writer (See her skits in Chapters 4 and 5). She prefers skits based on Bible stories, Bible verses, or concepts from the teachings of Jesus, and she always double-checks to be sure the Bible message comes through. "Never forget," she says, "that you perform for the glory of the Lord, not the glory of your clown character!"

Jelly Bean's Tips for Using Bible Skits

1. Study the skit's Scripture. The key to the clown's interpretation is a good working knowledge of the Scripture passage.

2. View it through the eyes of a clown.

3. Add your touch of uniqueness, but don't "clown it up" until the message is no longer theologically sound.

4. Read (or have someone else read) the Bible passage to the audience before or after the skit.

5. Practice! Practice! Practice!

See also *A Popcorn Stuff Seed* (page 206), *Parable of the Clown Talents* (page 162), and *Parable of the Nose of Great Price* (page 75) by Janet Tucker.

SPARKY

Trudy Cravatta-DiNardo is an assistant professor at a college in Pennsylvania and a communications trainer for personnel groups in business. She is a cantor and lector at her church (Catholic) and director of the high school youth group. Plus, she serves as adjudicator for intercollegiate forensics/speech tournaments. This is a very busy woman who is also a fire-eating clown minister with a resumé so long that at first glance you might think she's kidding — clowns are apt to do that! But Trudy's 12-year experience is, indeed, real. And no kidding about the fire-eating either. That's real, too! How in the world does she get it all done?

Obviously, she's well organized. Maybe that's because of her background as a teacher. Her subject areas — English, speech, writing, and drama — lend themselves well to clowning, too, since "communication" is what clowning is all about. In addition to fire-eating (That must communicate *something*!), her specialties as a clown are balloon sculpturing, mime, and puppetry. These skills she teaches, from time to time, in clown ministry workshops.

Trudy is a member of Clowns of America, Inc., and Phoenix Power and Light Company, an interfaith performing arts ministry organization for which she is currently chairperson of "Phoenix-on-the-Road," responsible for coordinating national day and weekend workshops.

As a clown minister, Trudy's first love is the healing ministry — nursing home residents, hospital patients, and developmentally disabled citizens. (Oh, yes, she also knows sign language, which can be very helpful in these situations.) One day, when her "Sparky" arrived to minister in a hospital, the head nurse told her that there was one patient whom she could not visit because of a head trauma injury. So Sparky (and the head nurse) visited other patients. Trudy says, "After seeing Sparky in action, the nurse asked me if I would visit the 'restricted' patient. I was nervous, because head trauma patients' reactions are unpredictable. I remembered, however, what the Reverend Bill Pindar once told me, 'Your clown stops becoming when you stop risking.' I entered the room and just 'clowned around' with the man. After I left the room, he got in a wheelchair and followed me throughout the wing. The nurses were quite surprised, because he had never wanted to leave his room."

And another time: "A friend, who is a nurse, asked me to come to the hospital to visit one patient, an elderly man who was very sick and did not have many visitors. When I entered his room, I found him to be a pleasant man, despite the many tubes hooked to his body. I took out an oil can and began to 'oil' his joints. He laughed and laughed, and pointed to his knees, saying, 'Give me more. Give me more.' I stayed with him a long time, then left him laughing. His wife was there in the room and followed me out. She was laughing and crying and said, 'He hasn't laughed for so long . . . He's dying of cancer.' I discovered that he died the next week."

Sparky's Tips for Healing Ministry

1. Always ask if there are some patients you will not be allowed to visit. Respect the restrictions.

2. Do not give food or water to patients.

3. Do not assist patients — call for a nurse if needed.

4. No more than two clowns in a room at a time.

5. Don't forget visitors and staff — clowns are for everyone, not just the residents.

See also *Mary's Baby Shower* (page 218) by Trudy Cravatta-DiNardo.

From left to right: Rusty, Strawberry, Jim and June Gorgans together.

RUSTY AND STRAWBERRY

Meet Jim and June Gorgans, "Rusty" and "Strawberry," a husband-and-wife clown ministry team from Florida. With several years of clowning under their baggy suits, they've had lots of experience, but one special opportunity makes them unique — they worked in a field medical tent (a MASH unit) in South Florida, with the victims of Hurricane Andrew.

Jim relates: "Throughout the day we were graciously thanked for the many smiles that appeared on the faces of patients who had to visit the medical tent. I remember a sad young man with a severely cut hand. As the surgeon cleaned and sutured the wound, I tried to help by telling the young man not to worry — unless the doctor asked 'Rusty' to finish up! It was then he smiled." They also made balloon animals, including "Jonah in the Whale," for children at a shelter, and visited people at the devastating sites of their homes in a destroyed neighborhood. Rusty's and Strawberry's oldest granddaughter, Julie, went with them as "Cherry the Clown." All three felt as touched and blessed by the experience as the folks to whom they ministered.

38

Jim is currently the Southeast Director of the World Clown Association and President-Elect of the Southeast Clown Association. He and June are members of the Telephone Pioneer Clown Corps and the Gainesville (Florida) Sunshine Clown Alley.

Jim was a magician called "Mr. Jim" who took his first clown training at a workshop where June was the teacher! Later he attended the Carpet Clown College in Ruskin, Florida. Both agree that continuing education is important and take advantage of workshops and educational opportunities whenever possible.

This team belongs to a Christian Missionary Alliance Church. "We love to share God's Word in church," says June. "We also minister in nursing homes, retirement centers, Bible schools, kids' clubs, hospitals, schools, conventions, and relief centers." June currently teaches a workshop on hospital and nursing home visitation.

Many of Jim's and June's props are made from items found in the home: Pots and pans for musical instruments, puppets made from plastic bottles and toilet seat covers, a growing tree made of rolled newspaper, a slate board for storytelling. They measure success in smiles, hugs, handshakes, and laughter — all of which they've had plenty!

Rusty's and Strawberry's "Good Business" Tip

Misunderstanding between customer (the hiring person or persons, including church personnel) and supplier (the clown) has caused many unnecessary heartaches. To protect both parties, prepare a contract that outlines exactly what is expected and what will be done. Be careful when customers say, "You know what I need." . . . You may know what they need, but you don't know what they *want*.

See also *Zack, the Whiz Kid* (page 193) by Jim and June Gorgans.

SWEET PEA

Most "real people" behind clown faces have experienced the harsh realities of life to some degree. They know what it means to survive. Kay "Sweet Pea" Turner is not only a survivor — she's a *winner*! Her story is poignant, memorable, and inspirational.

Ten years ago Kay was severely depressed, not in the least outgoing, and never wanted to call attention to herself — in short, seemingly the very last kind of person suited to be a clown. Yet, when the call went up, "Anyone interested in clowning . . .?" Kay didn't hesitate a minute. Now, ten years later, she is an active performer and clown teacher in her church and community and across the country.

Because of her battle with depression, she has an interesting perspective on nursing home ministry: "Not every clown is cut out of a mold that makes clowning in a nursing home right for them. I am one of those clowns. When I enter a nursing home, I feel clouds of depression around me from some of the residents who have had to give up their freedom and responsibility and now resent their situation. Personally, I find it very difficult to keep their heartaches and loneliness from entering me. Too many times I tried to force myself to visit nursing homes because I was told, 'It is what ministry clowns are supposed to do.' Nonsense! A clown should serve where his or her talents can be put to best use."

On the other hand, since Kay has reared two children, one of whom was born with cerebral palsy, she has no difficulty clowning for developmentally disabled or severely ill people. "Once when I was clowning for a group of disabled children in Canada," she says, "I was suddenly overcome with tears. I quickly left the group, thinking how terrible it was for a clown to cry, but a friend nearby encouraged me not to turn away, but rather to grow from the experience. Some clowns paint a tear on their faces to represent sorrow or empathy, but my tears were real, born of familiarity with the situations and problems of these children and their families. It was not grief I felt, but a release, because I had already been through so much with my own family. Since that day, my 'Sweet Pea' cries real tears of joy, sorrow, sympathy, or love. This is just another avenue of her growth that can be utilized to serve others."

Kay believes in continuing education and training for all clowns and in support group membership. She belongs to the Red Stick Slapsticks Clown Alley of Baton Rouge, Phoenix Power & Light Co., Inc., the World Clown Association, and Clowns of America International. She is also a member of the Clown Hall of Fame located in Delevan, Wisconsin. She lives in Louisiana and is an avid collector of clowning books, magazines, tapes, and paraphernalia.

A final story: Because she believes so strongly in growth, Kay occasionally visits nursing homes, even though they make her uncomfortable. These visits are as much for her as for the residents. "Once I visited an elderly, bedridden lady," she says. "She was blind, and we talked for a long time before I told her I was a clown. To my surprise, she became very excited. She told me that as a small child she had limited vision and had seen a clown in a circus. She never again saw another circus or another clown. I asked if she would like to 'see' me with her hands. What a wonderful time she had touching my face, my

41

nose, my hair! And she laughed heartily as I raised my big shoes to her bedside for her to touch. This lady's joy will be forever imprinted in my memories. A treasure."

Sweet Pea's Tips

1. Keep a log of skits, gags, ideas, and notes. This file can be invaluable when preparing a show, big or small.

2. A ministry clown is not limited to performing in a church setting. Choose other areas to be a blessing: Scouting events, public and private schools, civic events, private parties, business promotions, clubs, libraries, Special Children's Art Festivals, and Special Olympics.

3. I once heard someone say, "Clowns do things funny, but they don't necessarily do funny things." Apply this concept to whatever location you are working, and you will be successful.

See also *Follow the Yellow Brick Road* (page 241), and *Three Short Skits* (page 166) by Kay Turner.

MARKO

"Marko" was born in 1982 as a member of the Rockwell International Clown Unit. His real life counterpart is Mark Seckel, whose real life job is working in youth marketing for McDonald's restaurants in Ohio.

Of his first experience as a clown, Mark Seckel says, "I was instructed to powder down, but I wasn't sure how much I should powder. I thought a few grains would do it, but by the end of the evening I looked like I'd spent the night in a clothes dryer . . . melting!"

Nevertheless, he was hooked on clowning because of the love and joy of the children in the hospital where he'd had that first experience. After that he did parades, charity work, TV telethons, birthday parties, and management shows, but with the Rockwell Unit he was only averaging six appearances a month — not nearly enough for someone who'd been bitten hard by the "clown bug." Since he and his wife, Diane, were already involved with children's ministries in their church (an interdenominational congregation of 5,000 members), clown ministry was a logical next step.

Marko's first appearance in junior church was another milestone: "It lasted seven minutes and I did every trick I knew — twice! Again, the children were warm and friendly, but I knew I had to work harder if my ministry as a clown was going to be effective."

Mark Seckel's ministry *is* effective, because it is well planned and professionally delivered, and because he always interacts with his audience. Planning means time — time in study and time in prayer. Here is how one planning session went:

"As I meditated on I Corinthians 5:6, the Lord touched my heart. 'Don't you know that a little yeast works through the whole batch of dough?' The first thing I asked myself was, 'What is this saying?' In my own understanding, it tells me that a little of the wrong stuff can overrun that which is good. Or, 'A little bit (of the wrong stuff) is too much.' I thought about this for an entire week. Obviously, the Holy Spirit was dealing with me. How could Marko teach this to the children? Then one night I was mashing potatoes with an electric mixer when an idea came — wouldn't it be funny to see a continuous batch of something come from the mixer! So I mixed a solution of water and soap and let it sit until there were no bubbles in it at all. Then I turned the mixer on and it worked! I had a good supply of foam that quickly overran the bowl. How could I make it funnier? . . . If we let sin into our lives, it becomes difficult to control. What if I could not control the mixer? . . . I taped a 'dummy' electric cord to the mixer, obvious to the audience, then plugged it into an extension cord, again so the audience could see it. I even used a dummy on/off switch attached to the table the mixer was on. But the real power cord was hidden from the audience. Now my illustration was ready to go, but I needed to develop a story (the skit) so that Marko's actions made sense to the children and wouldn't be oversimplified. If a lesson is oversimplified, children will know what the blow off is before it happens. I also needed to work the lesson into the skit *without coming out of character and becoming a teacher.* After some thinking and writing (and rewriting) I had a new skit." (See "A Little Sin Is Too Much" on page 256).

Mark is a member of the World Clown Association, Clowns of America International, and the Fellowship of Christian Magicians. He is featured in the video, "To Pay the Price," a discussion of teenage morals and standards. In addition to his church clowning, he can be seen at community events, restaurants, and picnics. And he still does the occasional, all-important birthday party!

Marko's Tips for Success

1. Always acquire as much information as you can about where you are to be performing. Stage? Good PA system? Security? Waiting area? Accessible parking? Adult supervision for children? Even after making a list and a confirmation call, be prepared for anything. One time I was assured that a good PA was in place, but when I arrived, I found only one input. This meant the PA could not accommodate my tape player too. I was glad I had my own system with me!

2. Make all movements big and clowny. In a movie or video, the camera can focus in on movements, but on a stage the audience will not notice quick or small actions.

3. Watch your body placement at all times. When talking with another clown, both of you should be at least at a 45-degree angle to each other so that the audience can see most of your front. When gesturing, use the hand or foot farthest away from the audience to keep from hiding your face or body.

4. Don't get so wrapped up in the script that you miss opportunities to interact with the audience.

5. Entertain! The more entertaining something is, the more it will be remembered.

See also *A Little Sin Is Too Much* (page 256), *Mining for Gold* (page 106), and *Peer Pressure* (page 254) by Mark Seckel.

CHAPTER THREE

CLOWNS AROUND THE WORLD

Clown ministry as we know it today, beginning with the work of Floyd "Socataco" Shaffer in the 1960s, was chiefly an American phenomenon until the last decade. Now, though moving slowly, it reaches into other parts of the world. It is catching on particularly in Europe, where an organization called "Holy Fools, United Kingdom" has a current membership of nearly 200. Their roster, though mostly clowns of England, also includes clowns from Wales, Scotland, Germany, Switzerland, Israel, and Zimbabwe. In researching this book, other clown ministers were found in Australia, New Zealand, New Guinea, Ghana, and Puerto Rico (an American territory).

Blue Brattle, chairman of Clowns International, says that apart from the "Holy Fools," he has found no reference to clown *ministry* in his foreign membership list. "Which does not mean," he says, "that they don't do it. I just have no records that they do it." This is an indication that clown ministers around the world (and they *do* exist in growing numbers) need to join their professional organizations, as those in America do, or at least report their work to recording agencies, so that they can be located. This would also provide clown ministers outside the United States a network of encouragement to draw from.

There are differences between clown ministers working outside the United States and those within. They have a different sense of humor and a different style of performance. They seem to be more whimsical, more free-wheeling, than American clowns. Their skits (included in Chapters 4 and 5), though well structured, zip in and out of multiple cracks and crevices like low-flying crop dusters. (Never mind the *feather* dusters!) The author of this book found herself blinking in awe, just trying to keep up!

There is another style of make-up, too — in addition to Whiteface, Auguste, and Tramp — mostly prevalent in Europe (see Roly Bain, page 52). It's a delightfully refreshing, "less is more" application that lets the real face shine through. Carolyn Costley (page 21) is an American clown who has adopted this style. We have much to learn from our clown brothers and sisters overseas!

RAINBOW

When *The Clown Ministry Handbook* was writen in 1982, Philip Noble was rector of an Episcopal Church in Prestwick, Scotland, and one of the first working European clown ministers. Remarkably, he is still serving the same church. He is also commissioned as an evangelist and has the freedom to travel widely as "Rainbow," a silent clown who is very gentle and open to discovery. Last time we checked, Rainbow had discovered "soap bubble art" and its astonishing possibilities for ministry. (One of his soap bubble skits appears on page 252.) Originally, his specialties were *origami,* the Japanese art of paper-folding — "A crumpled piece of paper seems to fold itself into a bird" — and string art, an assortment of string figures collected during his travels through the remote areas of New Guinea. Now he has added more skills — rope art (We assume Rainbow discovered "big string"), storytelling, and juggling.

Rainbow shares mainly in the areas of spiritual renewal, worship, and healing. Philip says, "In the early days I found some situations arising where the pastor or leader had a particular idea of what a clown is and how he or she should act. This usually meant being funny and amusing the children. My clown is not really that kind. He is more a discoverer of the amazing creative possibilities that lie in even the simplest things." Maybe this is why Rainbow chooses to work with string, paper, and soap bubbles!

Over the past ten years, Philip has been invited to share in hundreds of different situations in many different countries. He finds no need to advertise, because invitations come through people or churches who have seen him elsewhere or know of him through others whose judgment they trust. This is one advantage of being part of a local church, and of staying in one place for such a long time.

"I now take special care to accept only those invitations that I feel comfortably in tune with," he says. He has found, oddly, that rather than narrowing the number of invitations, this screening process has increased them! Because of the growth of clown ministry across the United Kingdom, Philip is now able to refer churches and groups to other clown ministers according to their needs. This is a plus for him, and for the Kingdom — both "Kingdoms"!

In his ministry Philip is a respected teacher and lecturer on clowning, most recently at the European Conference in Sweden. He has also helped, twice, with Fuller Theological Seminary's Doctor of Ministries program in Los Angeles, California, using clown storytelling as a visual art. In the introduction to his book, *The Clown in Church,* Philip writes: "In each generation we must seek expressions of faith that are not stale copies or worn-out interpretations of previous years. Our task as Christians is to share the joy of the Gospel with the world, a world that is forgetting how to celebrate." *(The Clown in Church* by Philip Noble may be purchased from the Rev. Noble at 56 Ayr Road, Prestwick KA9 1RR, Ayrshire, Scotland.)

According to Philip, even mistakes can be opportunities for new ideas and growth, because the clown is graciously received. "Failure," he says, "seems to me to be only possible when we view success as getting things right. While not excusing lack of practice and preparation, I find the heart of the clown is of utmost importance."

Rainbow's Best Tips

1. Learn to juggle in 30 minutes: First, throw the balls without attempting to catch at all — work on height and direction. Then, add the catching. Learning will be quick, but development of the skill takes time and practice.

2. Everything from the first contact with the meeting place janitor to the final cleaning up of your own mess is part of being a clown minister. Some of the most powerful and effective moments can happen immediately prior to or following a time of clown ministry. Don't neglect these moments.

See also *Faith — A Gift of God* (page 252), *God Is* (page 227), *Ice Cream* (page 191), and *The Disappearing Varnish* (page 251) by Philip Noble.

ROLY

"I was only eight years old when I read Coco's biography. I finished reading it on a summer holiday, spent with my father in a caravan in Devon. Putting it down, I drew a picture of a clown and carefully inscribed in large letters underneath, 'I want to be a clown.'"

The next significant time that a clown entered Roly Bain's consciousness was at theological college when he needed to preach a sermon. "I had the vision of Jesus as Clown, and that was what I preached about. That was fifteen years ago, and I've pursued that capering, crucified Clown ever since."

He has preached, written, and broadcast about clowning, performed in cathedrals, prisons, churches, festivals, colleges, schools — anywhere and everywhere — and collected clown figurines and anything remotely relevant to the subject. "Having clown on the brain," he says, "is the worst place to have it!"

Roly Bain ("Roly") is an Anglican clergyman who, after years of trying to balance his job as Vicar of a parish in England with his call to Christian clowning, is now a full-time clown minister. He gave up his parish, and he and his wife and two small children moved to Bristol, where Roly became a student again — at Fool Time, the Circus School. He has nothing but deep respect and words of praise for Fool Time. "What the school enabled me to do," he says, "was to give me the confidence and the wherewithal not just to perform solo, but to go it alone." He has been full-time for over a year now and is doing extremely well.

Roly was one of the founders of Holy Fools, United Kingdom. He enjoyed working with the start-up, though he feels he did far too much organizing and administration. Now, he says, "I don't have to worry about organizing anyone but me!"

One of his fondest memories is of performing at Lichfield Cathedral at a day of celebration and pilgrimage: "There were about two thousand people packed in, and not only did we (the clowns) get them all pirouetting manically as a sign of repentance, we also got the distinguished line of twenty-four bishops from all over the Anglican Communion doing it as well! Now that's what I call a backdrop!"

Roly Bain is a professional, from his red nose to the red heart and cross on his big black shoes. He believes that "holy fools" need to be "clowny," to have good circus skills for presenting the Gospel. His particular skill, with which he credits the Fool Time Circus School, is walking the slackrope. From this he has developed some unique routines that are becoming his trademark:

"I have a lethal-looking, freestanding frame that looks impossibly precarious, with large crosses on either end. My favorite routine is 'The Slackrope of Faith.' There's all sorts of nonsense trying to get on the thing, with lines thrown in about it being wonderful once you're there. Once on, I cling to the cross for dear life till I get my balance, explaining that it's my slackrope of faith because it's narrow, wobbly, and risky, but quite exhilarating. I end up juggling hoops to show that with faith nothing is impossible. I finish with the line, 'This is the place to be, this is the place to dream, this is the place to dare, this is the place to play. This is the slackrope of faith. If you're foolish enough, you can try one for yourselves.' It's a routine that combines skill, comedy, foolishness, and truth. My task is simple — to entertain, to move, and to teach. When I can do all three at the same time, then I know I'm doing it right!"

Roly's Tips for Courage

1. If you make a mistake, or if there's an interruption from someone, just take it and use it, playing with what you're given. Stay in tune, not only with your own foolishness, but with the foolishness of others. It means being alive and alert to every opportunity.

2. Be prepared, but don't be too script-bound. Have the courage to produce stuff from deep inside you. That's where foolishness is found.

3. Remember that clowns are vulnerable lovers. Allow yourself to be vulnerable . . . and love.

Note: Roly is currently under contract with HarperCollins Publishers to write a book about his call to Christian clowning. *Fools Rush In* will present the uniquely European perspective. Watch for it!

See also *Honest Ananias* (page 173), *Remember Me* (page 79), and *Rocky the Rock* (page 260) by Roly Bain.

From left to right: Archie and Bombin, otherwise known as Carlos Sanchez (top) and Rafael Rondon (bottom).

BOMBIN AND ARCHIE

Rafael "Bombin" Rondon and Carlos "Archie" Sanchez are Spanish-speaking clown ministers from Puerto Rico. Though they began their ministry individually (Rafael started clowning when he was seven years old!), they have been working together for nearly three years and now consider themselves an inseparable team.

According to J. T. Sikes (page 17), Rafael and Carlos won everyone's hearts at the 1992 Clown Convention with their endearing skits and their illuminating joy in the Lord. They glowed, and the glow was catching!

Their ministry is chiefly in churches and Christian schools, including schools for the hearing impaired, but they also do birthdays. And, naturally, they are much sought after for Spanish-speaking clown ministry seminars.

Both are members of Clowns of America International and have won various convention awards, including Tramp, Multiple Balloons, Single Balloon, Group Skit, and Paradability.

Carlos is married and the father of two children; Rafael is single. Because of the language barrier, the difficulty in communicating, this author fears that some of the charm of this team may be lost in translation. Rafael says, "Sometimes I mess verbs and nouns." But he does it so delightfully! The characters of Bombin and Archie are best seen in their material, some of which appears in Chapters 4 and 5.

Bombin's and Archie's Tip:

Don't be afraid to adapt skits to suit your situation. Add more clowns. Take away clowns. Make it work for you.

See also *Sticky Chair* (page 125) and *The Banana Illusion* (page 236) by Rondon & Sanchez.

VALENTINE

Olive Drane is a Scottish homemaker who describes her work, before becoming a clown, as "very ordinary." What is *not* ordinary is her call to Christian clowning, and this is best told in her own words (condensed here):

"I was going about my work when suddenly, and certainly unexpectedly, I heard a laugh. Instinctively, I looked 'round to see who had crept up on me. But there was no one there. I was alone — and very surprised. For I soon realized that I was the one who was laughing.

"The last time I had even smiled was longer ago than I could possibly remember. Following the death of my second child, life seemed to have little meaning, and the platitudes of Christian friends often made things worse, not better. I felt as if I were falling helplessly down some dark mine shaft that just went on and on and on. And then, I laughed. I can't even remember exactly what I was laughing about. But it was as if a pinprick of light had at last appeared in the darkness of my life . . . and I finally sensed that there might be some hope.

"I knew I needed to respond to this unexpected display of God's love, and I found myself saying, 'Well, God, if there's anything you'd like me to do, just say the word.' Imagine my astonishment when God said, 'Actually, Olive, I'm looking for a clown just now.' I had secretly hoped that God might want me to become somebody truly useful in the community. But a clown?! God definitely has a sense of humor. And so, after many conversations with this delightful God, I agreed to give it a try.

"As I applied white make-up to my face for the first time, I certainly empathized with the imagery of the death mask. The recent experiences that had torn apart my own life were still too vivid to forget. But gradually, God introduced me to the colors of life, and together we started to paint my face . . . And so Valentine came to life."

Olive has shared that story with hundreds of people in different parts of the world — in coffee houses, as an after-dinner speaker, in workshops, exhibitions, and many times in church services. As she tells it, she chooses the colors from her make-up box, paints her face, and changes her clothes, gradually changing from Olive into Valentine.

"Whenever I share my own journey of faith like this," Olive says, "there is always someone who finds that it addresses deep personal needs. In particular, those who have suffered the loss of a child, or have been abused in some way, find this gives them the opportunity to talk and begin a journey of healing. And this in turn is bringing further healing and growth to me."

Valentine is a silent clown because "it's safer." But that doen't mean it's easier. The language of mime, as Olive says, demands careful preparation and thought. "Sacrificing the use of words makes both the artist and the audience more attentive to what is happening." Olive recently led a whole service in mime for one of the presbyteries of the Church of Scotland. What a challenge! Just the fact that they invited her to do it makes an interesting comment on the openness of so many of the Scottish churches to this type of ministry.

Valentine's Tips From the Heart

1. Be open to the world, the people around you.

2. As a clown, show your weakness and vulnerability.

3. Come alongside others, sharing joys, pains, or whatever, and in the process, point to Jesus.

4. In the Gospels, Jesus always affirms people and lifts them up. It is important for a Christian clown never to put people down by making them look stupid or by getting them to make mistakes.

5. Jesus is the Christian clown's source of creativity, as well as a perfect model of mission and inspiration.

See also *Newspapers for Prayer* (page 132), *The Dancing Clown* (page 258), and *United Communion* (page 81) by Olive Drane.

Chad and Valerie Ashcroft

Stephen and Godwin Ashcroft

Ludo the Clown, Lulubelle, Lotto and Swank

LUDO THE CLOWN
(with LULUBELLE, LOTTO, and SWANK)

Stephen Ashcroft, his wife Valerie, and sons Godwin and Chad form a neat little family troupe of clowns in London, England. "Clowning," Stephen says, "is almost the only activity all four of us take part in together!" They're fortunate, as so many families with growing children are pulled in different directions these days.

Even so, Stephen and Valerie are both busy people. They are teachers. Valerie ("Lulubelle") lectures in college and is a local preacher in the Methodist Church; Stephen, in addition to his teaching, is a local politician — a past Deputy Mayor of the London Borough of Merton. His "Ludo the Clown" was born to help advertise Christian Aid. Since 1990 he has edited *Foolish Times*, the newsletter of Holy Fools, United Kingdom; Valerie is treasurer of the same organization. The boys ("Lotto" and "Swank"), of course, have busy lives as students.

Then how, and why, do they find time for clown ministry? Well, the Ashcrofts *make* time, because they like being together, and they enjoy clowning. (They're also *very good* at it!)

One evening, however, after a clowning service, a woman said to them, "I enjoyed the service, but I'm not sure we're supposed to enjoy worship." This raised an important issue for Stephen: "If we Christians don't enjoy worship, why should we expect others to join us in it . . . and how will we ever be able to endure eternity?"

Stephen and his family believe it is important to give as much emphasis to the word "clown" as to the word "ministry." For them, an ideal skit is evenly balanced between religious theme and clown routine, and is firmly rooted in both — the religion informs the clowning, the clowning embodies the religion. " 'Bolt-on' clowning," says Stephen, "is no more acceptable than 'bolt-on' Christianity."

According to Stephen, clowning seems to have something peculiarly relevant to say about Christianity's attitude toward human vulnerabilities and absurdities. Specifically: "Christ came for all, Whiteface as well as Auguste. Laurel stands as much in need of redemption and salvation as does Hardy. To some extent, the vulnerable little man and the bossy, domineering know-all are present in everyone. So, while our family tries to use the clown hierarchies properly, we also often seek to end on a note of reconciliation and interdependence between Whiteface and Auguste. 'Paul in Prison' (see page 230) is a good example of this."

As clown ministers, the Ashcroft family's aims are best summed up in a statement made by a man who had just witnessed a service in which they had taken part. He said, "You didn't teach me anything new, but you made me listen again." Unfortunately, the basic messages of Christianity are so familiar these days that it takes something out of the ordinary to make people "listen again." Thank God for out-of-the-ordinary clown ministers!

Ludo's Tips on Writing and Using Sketches (Skits)

1. Produce skeletons, which can be fleshed out in rehearsal. Cooperative effort gets the best results.
2. When performing a sketch, regard it as a route map, not a wheelchair.

61

3. Audience participation helps ensure that people are listening properly.

See also *Paul in Prison* (page 230), *The Beatitudes* (page 188), and *The Resurrection* (page 151) by Stephen Ashcroft.

DENNIS CLARE, Performing Artist

Dennis Clare is an Australian who performs without the "clown name" we have come to expect. This is, perhaps, because he is a man of many skills — clowning, mime, acting, dance, and even trapeze! — which he uses separately or in combination, either as a soloist or in collaboration with dancers, musicians, and other performing artists. In all of this he sees himself as an entertainer, deriving his definition of the word "entertain" from its Greek meaning: "to suspend." For Dennis, it is *to suspend between heaven and earth.*

As a clown and mime, Dennis seeks to reaffirm humanness. He says, "So many aspects of the world we live in are geared to coldly ripping values away. I want to give back warmth and joy."

Dennis portrays the clown as someone who puts himself in the position of underdog, without being anyone's fool. "I'm not going to be sold the town clock," he says. His clown is still in control, but rather than put other people down, he chooses that position for himself. He enables laughter without hurting, allows the release of pent-up pressure, like the valve on a pres-

63

sure cooker. "This," he says, "is the fine tradition that Charlie Chaplin took to Hollywood. But in movies thereafter it was tainted, becoming only shallow slapstick. For many street performers today, it is unfortunately lost in the Middle Ages."

Part of Dennis's journey is to bring that clown home, to give an Australian face and a contemporary feeling to an art form that can be deeply relevant without being stupid or quaint.

For 15 years Dennis has performed in a wide variety of contexts: Television, stage, concerts, conferences, festivals, schools, and workshops. His unique ministry has taken him to Holland, England, Poland, Mexico, the United States, and all over Australia, including the World Expo at Brisbane. "I love to wander amongst people," he says, "and create spontaneous entertainment. I also enjoy conferences where I must work to a theme. And I always welcome the role of advisor or teacher. There's a certain freedom in versatility."

A Good Tip From Dennis

Work sometime in a place where people don't expect to see a clown. For instance, I have gone into hotels with the musicians "Glass Canoe." Hotels provide a common meeting place for the rock generation, but one where they don't expect to see a clown, particularly one who knows their language. To see such an audience turn to the clown is a real delight.

See also *God's Gift Shop* (page 248) by Dennis Clare.

CLOWNBO

Tommy Thomson is a Scottish clown who calls himself a "professor of balloonology." He is an expert at crafting shapes out of balloons, and there are 40-some shapes in his permanent repertoire. "If I need a prop — hammer, ladder, animal, whatever," he says, "I make it out of balloons. Everything I do and have is God's, for he revealed the wonderful, creative gift of balloonology in me."

Tommy's first clown person was a Whiteface named "Pulpit," but neither Tommy nor Pulpit was entirely happy with that arrangement. One evening after a church clowning event, Tommy stopped at the local fish and chip shop for supper, still made-up and outfitted as Pulpit. "Several youths were there and started poking fun at me," he relates. "They were shouting out various names — some unrepeatable! — but one name they shouted was 'Clownbo,' probably because the film 'Rambo' had recently been in the cinemas. 'Clownbo' — I liked it! God had supplied my name in a most unusual way. I consider it a special baptism, a sign of God's approval." With the new name also came a new face, as he changed to an Auguste clown.

In the early days of his clowning, most of the bookings Tommy received were referred by the Reverend Philip "Rainbow" Noble (see page 49), his first clown teacher. As he became better known, he began receiving direct bookings to many different and out-of-the-way places. Because of his work as an Administration Assistant with British Rail Property Board, he is able to travel anywhere in Britain and Europe at little or no cost and also enjoys travel concessions in many countries around the world.

So Clownbo travels. And he travels at a cost anyone can afford — a donation. "I don't want anyone to be denied the opportunity of my services due to finances. I am not in the ministry for financial gain. If my expenses can be covered, then I am satisfied; if not, then I am still grateful for the opportunities presented to me. My main purpose is to make people aware of God's transforming power through the figure of this holy fool, Clownbo. The day someone says they can't afford me is the day I give up clowning, because for me, 'the price has already been paid.' "

In his recent travels, Tommy was part of the "Love Europe" mission, which enabled him to share the Good News all over Europe. During that time he took a week's training in Offenburg, Germany, then went on to Nantes, France, where he led a team on street clowning. Tommy's Clownbo seems to be happiest as a walkabout clown, meeting and mixing with people in street situations.

Tommy is a member of Holy Fools, United Kingdom, and also of a small, unique group called "Omega" — an actor, a musician, a mime, and a clown (Clownbo) — who all operate individual ministries but also come together to perform as a group. They specialize in working with children and youth, and in conducting workshops.

Tommy has been featured on BBC's "The Quest," ITV's "God's Reps," and on "Surprise, Surprise," a show broadcast throughout Britain. In addition to his full-time job and all of his activities, Tommy is a Methodist lay preacher who conducts three to four services per quarter. "Sometimes that guy with the red nose pops up as a 'divine interrupter,' " he says. "Other times it's just me."

Clownbo's Tips on Books and on the Big Mistake

1. If you're interested in balloon sculpture, Ralph Dewey's *Good News Balloons* is an excellent reference. His balloon sculptures always look close to the real thing. The book may be purchased from Dewey at 1110 E. Princeton, Deer Park, TX 77536.

2. It was through the clown's "other Bible" — *The Clown Ministry Handbook* by Janet Litherland (Meriwether Publishing Ltd., copyright © 1982) — that I developed a strong theological understanding of the Christ-like clown figure that I was becoming. I recommend it. (And this author certainly appreciates the recommendation!)

3. Learn from my mistake: One of the earliest bookings I did, for a Church of Scotland's children's group, almost brought my ministry to an abrupt end. I made the mistake during one of my routines. I asked for a volunteer to help me out, whereupon around 30 to 35 children swamped onto the platform and ransacked my stuff! One learns a lot from disasters such as that. I certainly did.

See also *It's in the Air* (page 134), *Mine!* (page 97), *Seeing Is Believing* (page 155), and *Wise and Foolish Builders* (page 242) by Tommy Thomson.

KUJO

"Kujo" is the Ghanaian clown name of an American minister, Tim Morrison. Tim, perhaps, belongs in Chapter 2, "Clowns Across America," but Kujo, because of his Ghanaian roots, belongs here, with "Clowns Around the World." This author didn't have the heart to separate Tim and Kujo!

Among West African people, babies are named for the day of the week on which they are born. They are then given official names in a naming ceremony on the eighth day of life, but continue to carry, in some fashion, the "day name" for the rest of their lives. Tim's clown person was born on a Monday, and male babies born on Monday among the Ewe people are called Kudzo, which is pronounced Kujo. Tim says, "I kept the Ghanaian spelling until I moved to Georgia in 1991, when I reverted to the phonetic spelling. Kudzo, written out, looked too much like "kudzu," a fast-growing, prolific, nuisance vine that swallows up roadsides and trees in the South!"

Though Tim is now a United Church of Christ pastor in the United States, he feels greatly influenced by his time spent as a missionary in Ghana. Even more than that, he was able to gather some interesting information on the clown in African culture — the clown is there, but not at all like the familiar creature we know and love. In Tim's own words:

"Masquerades are sometimes the African equivalent of a clown. A full mask, rather than facial make-up, enables the participant to act out a different, often comic, persona. Whiteface usually connotes the spirit world, rather than anything comic. In certain non-masquerade phenomena, such as possession dances, there is much clowning, sometimes a trifle obscene. Both 'possession' and a 'mask' free people from the restraints of ordinary life.

"There are some curious offshoots. I attended some church anniversary celebrations and a funeral for a paramount queen mother. At each of these gatherings, I noticed individuals — usually men but at the funeral, women — dressed rather poorly and obviously intentionally so. They were not only shabby but verging on the comical. To me it was like a combination of Freddy Freeloader and the Wizard of Oz Tin Man! I learned that these people are called *asafo*. They are usually the young men of a village, whose task is to protect the village chief, and, if necessary, to be warriors in tribal warfare. In public gatherings they dress purposely to stand out, and although they are not seen as "clowns," they make very definite attempts to bring laughter to the people. A queen mother has her equivalent to everything that a chief has; hence, there are women *asafo*. However, these women would never go to war.

"The *asafo* I have seen have always had some kind of paint on their faces. Ocher, for the Ewe people, is a sign of mourning. Some mourners streak it on themselves and others; some wear elaborate body designs, which they put on with "stamps." Similar body decoration in white is worn only by women and is a sign of merriment and rejoicing — often used at the birth of a child.

"As the time came for us to leave Ghana, the villagers held a celebration in which they dabbed our arms with white paint — a sign of celebration to recognize the achievement of a particularly difficult task or significant accomplishment."

Oddly, Tim wrote his first clown skit before he became a "real" clown. That skit enjoys a certain amount of fame now among solo clowns in many corners of the world, and this author is pleased to offer it on page 147. "Jedidiah Becomes a Clown" — the coming alive of a true clown — turned out, years later, to be the story of Kujo, when Kujo came alive in Tim Morrison.

Before Kujo, Tim tried being a Whiteface, but he was never comfortable, because his moustache stuck out. Kujo, however, is a happy, moustachioed Auguste, with a most unique look. He is silent and loves to "work the crowd" as an evangelist at schools, parades, prom parties, and civic events.

Kujo's Tip for Parades and Crowd Work

This comes straight out of a bad experience: Work apart from the secular clowns, because you never know what one of them will do. It might be something that will reflect badly on you and your ministry.

Tim, like other busy people, feels the frustration of wanting to "clown and clown and clown," but work and schedule constraints limit those opportunities. He worries about others like him, who take clowning seriously and approach clowning professionally, but who might be missing precious moments of a special kind of sharing, because there just aren't enough hours in each day. Those clowns are out there in larger numbers than we might care to admit. "What kinds of clowning do they do," Tim asks, "and *when*? Where do they go when the 'well runs dry?' How do they maintain their eagerness, their excitement?" . . . Is anyone talking?

See also *Jedidiah Becomes a Clown* (page 147) by Tim Morrison.

Part II:

EVERYTHING NEW

75 Original Clown Skits For Special Days

CHAPTER FOUR

SKITS FOR CLOWNING AROUND

Holy Days and Holidays

The skits in this chapter and the next are as wildly different as the clown ministers themselves — from silly and secular to sublimely sacred, and all manner of nonsense in between! Don't look for a Bible verse or "universal truth" in each skit. Some are written and performed only for good clean fun. Many of the "special day" skits can also be used at any time during the year. For example: "Right Now, God?" (National Procrastination Week) is about answering God's call. And "Free Love" (Valentine's Day) is about God's love — no strings attached.

Because each clown minister offers his or her own material, the skits also differ in style. Some skits preach sermons without apology and hammer the points home; others are so subtle one may well wonder if they *have* points! ("Did you get it, Mom?") All, however, represent what clown ministry is actually doing, *successfully,* in different kinds of situations and in different parts of the world. And, many of the skits were written by the author of this book, who appreciates all kinds of clowns and loves them dearly!

In the case of European clowns, language moves with a special, *delightful* flow, spiced with "chaps," "lads," "vicars," "torches," "sunshades," and other words that will give Americans pause. No changes were made in language (some words are explained), but American spellings and punctuation have been used to keep the form of the book more or less standard.

The drawings in these chapters were provided by the clown ministers and, in many cases, are caricatures of their own clown persons.

Some clowns finish their skits with a "round off," some call it a "click." Others call their endings the "blow off." Regardless of what it's called, it is the finish, ending, wrap-up, or main point of a skit.

Enjoy!

Parable of the Nose of Great Price

by Janet Tucker
(Jelly Bean)

CAST: Two CLOWNS

PROPS: Pipe cleaners (one for everyone in the audience); small table; sign with "Trading Post Now Open" on one side and "For God so loved the world that he gave his only begotten son" on the other side; various clown items (balloons, large clown glasses and scissors); several clown noses; mirror; trunk with clown props, magic tricks, balls for juggling, etc; box labeled "With Love From God," containing a clock, fake money, sheet music, a loaf of French bread, and a bottle of wine or container of grape juice.

OPENING: CLOWN 1 distributes colored pipe cleaners to audience as CLOWN 2 introduces the lesson.

CLOWN 2: Today we are going to talk about important things. We all know what things are important — homes, families, jobs, special hobbies. In Matthew 13:45-46, Jesus told a very small parable about something that is of large importance: "Again, the kingdom of heaven is like a merchant looking for fine pearls. When he found one of great value, he went away and sold everything he had and bought it." (NIV) Now notice in the story that the person didn't just say, "Wow! That's a great pearl. I'd like to have it!" or "Maybe someday I can have a pearl that nice." Instead he made a sacrifice for it, gave up something really important to him, because the pearl was the most important thing in his priorities. We all have to make priority decisions every day concerning money, time, schedules, relationships, and so on.

Now then, everybody understands about important things, so take the pipe cleaner you have been given and take a moment right now to design that pipe cleaner into the most important thing in the world to you. Maybe a rectangle, if money is important; maybe the shape of a car, if that's important to you; maybe a round circle to represent a pizza, if that's what turns you on. Do your design now, and then just hold it till later in the service.

(CLOWNS 1 and 2 walk Off-stage, then CLOWN 1 re-enters with a small table and a sign, "Trading Post Now Open." Puts various clown items on table — balloons, large clown glasses, large clown scissors. Include several kinds of clown noses and a mirror.)

CLOWN 2:   *(Enters with no clown nose on.)* **Now you're all ready and so am I, ready to do a worship service in clown ministry.**

CLOWN 1:   **Sorry, I can't do anything with you. You're not a real clown.**

CLOWN 2:   **Yes I am! Look at my funny hair, my bright clothes, my large shoes!**

CLOWN 1:   **Sorry, you may be dressed up, but you're not a real clown. Clowns always have a big, red nose.**

CLOWN 2:   *(Looks in mirror, sees no nose, and gets upset. Covers nose with hand.)* **Oh, no, a naked nose!**

CLOWN 1:   *(Motions to trading post.)* **I've got a trading post here with some big, red noses that would look just fabulous with your outfit.** *(CLOWN 2 gazes at them hopefully.)* **Go ahead, try one on.**

CLOWN 2: *(Trying on nose, looking in mirror)* **I love it! How much?**

CLOWN 1: **One hundred dollars.**

CLOWN 2: *(Incredulous)* **A hundred dollars?** *(CLOWN 2 is discouraged, then suddenly has an idea. He gets into his clown trunk and begins to bring out props, magic tricks, juggling balls, etc., demonstrating them to the audience, then trading them in to CLOWN 1 in order to raise enough money to buy a nose. Finally nothing more is left to trade, and CLOWN 2 gets very dejected. He notices his name tag with his clown identity.)*

CLOWN 2: **This is all I have left — it's me, myself, my whole identity, but without the nose, nothing else is important, so I guess I'll give everything I have.**

CLOWN 1: **You'd really give up** *everything* **for this nose?** *(CLOWN 2 nods.)* **Wow. I'll tell you what — I'll let you have this nose on sale. How does ten cents sound?**

CLOWN 2: **You mean it?**

CLOWN 1: **Uh-huh.**

CLOWN 2: **That's great!** *(CLOWN 2 pays CLOWN 1 and takes off name tag to give to him.)* **Here.**

CLOWN 1: **No — you keep it.**

CLOWN 2: **Hey, thanks!** *(While CLOWN 2 puts on the nose and checks out his reflection in the mirror, CLOWN 1 turns over the Trading Post sign to read the back.)*

CLOWN 1: **"For God so loved the world, that he gave his only begotten Son . . ."** (John 3:16, KJV)

CLOWN 2: **When something is very important to us, we sacrifice everything . . .**

CLOWN 1: *(Brings out box labeled "With Love From God" and takes out clock.)* **God gives us time, that we might use it to further his kingdom.**

CLOWN 2: *(Takes out play money bills.)* **God gives us money, that we might help those in need.**

CLOWN 1: *(Takes out sheet music.)* **God gives us talents,**

that we might use them in his service.

CLOWN 2: *(Takes out a loaf of French bread and bottle of wine or container of grape juice. Communion bread is prepared as he speaks.)* **This is God's most precious gift to you. Reflect on the sacrifice Christ made just for you, that you might believe on his name. Come and receive the bread and the cup, and when you come, bring with you the symbol of the thing you fashioned from the pipe cleaner — the thing that is most important to you, and, in return for his gift, offer this to him on the altar as you commune.**

(CLOWN 2 offers the "Nose of Great Price" on the altar as a symbol of giving the clown for God's service. Others come forward to commune.)

Remember Me

Based on John 6 and 7

by Roly Bain
(Roly)

CAST: One CLOWN

PROPS: Bread roll, mug, wine to fill mug, broomstick, large bag or trunk containing three more bread rolls, communion elements for congregants.

SETTING: Sanctuary; bag is visible, center. (NOTE: Protect carpet where wine will spill.)

OPENING: CLOWN does the "tearing up newspaper" gag to set himself up for failure.

(Take an ordinary piece of newspaper, tear it in half, in half again, and so on. As you tear, count the pieces aloud and inaccurately: "Now I have two. [Tear] Now there are three — no, four? Five!" Be unable to do the sums [Count the pieces], so the children will count for you. In frustration, ask for magic words to make the pieces disappear. Everybody has to shout words together. Throw the pieces up in air, shouting "The newspaper has disappeared," and look suitably shame-faced as bits float down around you.)

CLOWN: *(Picks up bread roll, mug and broomstick.)* **Eat, drink, and be merry, they said.** *(Balances mug on stick, fills it, then lets it fall and spill. Tears up bread in lots of pieces to try and make it disappear; asks for magic words. It's still there . . .)* **This is my body, he said. However much you break it, it will not disappear. Eat it and remember me.** *(Congregants eat. Picks up mug.)* **This is my blood. Drink it and remember me.** *(Congregants drink. CLOWN stands cruciform.)* **I may look like an idiot. Actually, I'm a fool, a real fool, and I know the foolishness of God is greater than any human**

wisdom. In a little while you shall not see me, but I have not disappeared. In a little while you shall see me again. *(Climbs into bag/trunk. Then, comes out of bag/trunk and juggles three bread rolls.)* **I am the Bread of Life. You need never hunger, you need never thirst. Only believe and have eternal life.** *(Balances roll on stick.)* **All shall be raised on the last day.**

(Audience sings "I Am the Bread of Life" by Suzanne Toolan [copyright © 1971 by GIA Publishing, 7404 South Mason Avenue, Chicago, IL 60638] — or other appropriate hymn — as CLOWN exits, still balancing roll.)

United Communion

by Olive Drane
(Valentine)

OLIVE'S BACKGROUND NOTES: I have worked a few
times recently on international Schools of Evangelism for
the World Council of Churches, and this sketch came out
of that involvement, and the need to apply myself to understanding people of different theological and ethnic
backgrounds — to hear what they were really saying. This
mime sketch gives an opportunity to highlight our denominational idiosyncrasies, the things that we take for
granted, but which can so easily take over and have a
central place in our Christian worship and witness. The
aim of this skit is to recapture the heart of the gospel. It
is all done in mime.

MIME SKETCH: **Several clowns**
enter with their differently
sized and shaped bags — suit-
case, briefcase, gladstone bag,
etc. — from which they begin to
unpack their portable com-
munion kits. They each rep-
resent a different denomination,

and the contents of each bag emphasize the distinc-
tive aspects of the way that particular tradition be-
haves and believes, especially the ways they cele-
brate communion. Presbyterians have their small
cups and neatly sliced squares of bread; Catholics
have their wafers and incense; Baptists their grape
juice; Episcopalians, Methodists, and others may
also be featured, depending on the audience. Each
one sets up own equipment and begins to mime his
or her distinctive ritual.

   Through the door comes a holy fool — mirror-

ing Jesus — dressed very simply, and carrying only a rucksack. This clown is surprised and interested, as he or she inspects what each of the others is doing. Clown lacks all the necessary credentials to share any of the others' communion services, but still invites the others to join in a circle on the floor. Clown unpacks the rucksack, and shares its simple contents: Bread and wine.

CONCLUSION: The sketch may end there. Or, the Jesus figure can pack all the fancy equipment belonging to the others into the rucksack, leaving everyone united around the simple symbols he/she has brought.

A Daisy of a Year

by Janet Litherland

CAST: HAPPY (monolog) clown; SAD (silent) clown.

PROPS: Large artificial daisy; specialty act, clown song-book, three balls, two balloons.

OPENING: SAD is alone, seated on a bench, center.

(HAPPY enters, approaches SAD, holds out a daisy, and speaks.)

HAPPY: **Have a daisy. Happy New Year! What a beautiful day!** *(SAD shakes head, refusing flower.)* **What's the matter? This has been a daisy of a year, and the new year's gonna be even better. I've given away a daisy a day for three hundred and sixty-five days. I make everyone happy!** *(SAD looks at him, then looks away. HAPPY discards his daisy and prepares to do something cheerful — juggling, magic — whatever his specialty.)*
     Now, look here. I can even make *you* happy. *(He does his act, but SAD does not respond. HAPPY sits down beside SAD.)* **Come on now, nothing's that bad. You like music?** *(SAD shrugs. HAPPY pulls songbook from pocket, opens it and begins to sing badly, "Oh, What a Beautiful Morning." [From* Oklahoma! *by Rodgers and Hammerstein, copyright © 1943, Williamson Music, Inc., New York, NY. Available at your local music store.] SAD covers his ears.)* **You don't like that song? Here, you pick one.** *(Hands book to SAD. SAD turns a few pages and gives it back, pointing.)* **"Raindrops Keep Fallin' on My *Head*?" What kinda song is that? That doesn't sound cheerful.** *(Puts book on floor.)*
     Look here. Let me help you. You say you've

had a bad year? *(SAD nods, hugs himself, and shakes, indicating cold.)* **You're cold?** *(SAD pantomimes no, that people were cold toward him.)* **Oh, *people* were cold toward you. Wasn't anybody friendly?** *(No)* **Did you make anyone happy?** *(SAD shrugs.)* **Did you try?** *(Yes)*

Well, here, stand up. *(They both stand.)* **Let's see you juggle.** *(Gives SAD three balls. SAD juggles badly and balls fall.)* **OK, how about balloons?** *(Gives SAD a balloon to blow up, while HAPPY blows up his own. HAPPY succeeds and ties his; SAD fails.)*

Fiddlin' frogs! You really do have problems! Take mine *(Hands it over)* **and make an animal; a frog would be nice.** *(SAD tries, but pops the balloon. HAPPY throws his hands in the air.)* **What *can* you do?** *(Nothing)* **But you're a *clown*. You're supposed to make people happy!**

(SAD nods sadly, then picks songbook up off floor and turns pages. Holds it out to HAPPY.) **"Kum Ba Yah?"** *(SAD nods.)* **That means "come by here, my Lord."** *(SAD nods vigorously and pantomimes for the audience to sing.)* **You want us to ask the Lord to . . . come by here? To help?** *(SAD is exicted now.)* **OK, we can do that. We can sing "Kum Ba Yah" for you.** *(To audience:)* **Can't we?** *(Encourages response, then leads audience in all verses — crying, singing, praying — as SAD endearingly pantomimes each one. ["Kum Ba Yah" is in-cluded in* Mel Bay's Sunday School Song Book *by Pamela Cooper Bye, copyright © 1983 Mel Bay Publications, Inc., Pacific, MO. It also appears in many other songbooks.] At close of song, SAD is animated and happy . . . and giving out hugs.)*

(HAPPY puts arm around SAD's shoulder and indi-cates audience.) **Would you look at those smiles out there? Just look at them! I guess we've all felt the work of the Lord. That was a wonderful idea! Know**

84

what? You don't have to do funny things — just share yourself, the real person inside. That makes people happy, too.

So what's it going to be like for you in the New Year? Will you still be sad? *(No)* Will you let people love you just the way you are? *(Yes)* Is that your New Year's resolution? *(SAD looks at him questioningly.)* Resolution. That means a promise to yourself. *(SAD nods yes!)*

(HAPPY retrieves his daisy and once again offers it to SAD.) In that case, make it a daisy of a year! *(SAD takes daisy, hugs HAPPY, then passes daisy on to a child in audience.)*

The Very Best New Year's Resolution

Based on Ephesians 6:11 and adapted from Storytelling From the Bible *by Janet Litherland, copyright © 1991, Meriwether Publishing Ltd.*

by Janet Litherland

CAST: NARRATOR, "WEARER" clown (barefoot), "PROP" clown.

PROPS: (All homemade clown props — use cardboard, foil, paint, colorful ribbons, etc.) Breastplate of bronze, chain mail vest, bronze helmet, pair of greaves (shin guards), wooden shield covered with canvas and hide, arrows, can of pitch (anything gooey), a match (can be pantomimed if illustration is not safe for performance area), a double-edged sword, two javelins, belt, clown shoes, set of walkie-talkies. Also the following paper signs with sticky tape on the back: "Truth," "Righteousness," "Peace," "Faith," "Salvation," "Word."

OPENING: NARRATOR is Stage Left; CLOWNS enter from right, dragging a huge, brightly painted box containing all the props. As NARRATOR reads, PROP CLOWN dresses the WEARER in the appropriate props, except for the vest, which he puts on himself. CLOWNS take time putting on props, milking for laughs — props go on crooked, helmet falls over eyes, etc.

NARRATOR: Back in Bible times, a Roman soldier needed a lot of equipment when he went into battle. Over his clothing he wore a breastplate made of bronze to protect his heart . . . If he were a rich man, he wore, instead, a vest made of chain mail . . . He also wore a bronze helmet . . . and a pair of greaves, which protected his legs from knee to ankle . . . For defense, he carried a wooden shield covered with canvas and hide . . . This was very good against a favorite weapon, arrows that had been tipped with pitch . . . and set on fire (*Illustrate only if safe to do so*)

. . . because the arrows would burn themselves out in the tough hides . . . For offense, the soldier kept a double-edged sword at his thigh . . . and two javelins in his hands.

The soldier would put on all of his equipment except the helmet and sword . . . *(WEARER gives back helmet, with difficulty because he is clumsy, and sword, indicating that the CLOWN who gave them to him too soon is a dummy.)* The custom was for these two items to be handed to him by someone else.

What a wonderful word picture this makes! . . . *(PROP CLOWN indicates to audience, aside, that it's a wonderful picture, indeed — a stupid one.)* The writer of Ephesians used this picture to urge Christians to "arm" themselves against Satan. He also added a belt . . . and shoes . . . to the uniform.

Now imagine yourself as the soldier. You are wearing a breastplate *(PROP CLOWN indicates each piece)* . . . belt . . . and greaves. You are carrying a shield . . . and two javelins . . . This time you'll coat the pieces of equipment with "sealer," the powerful stuff that God gives to everyone. It's free! *(CLOWNS react to "free" with smiles and "whew!" gestures.)*

The belt you'll seal with Truth. *(PROP CLOWN slaps signs onto the following appropriate spots.)* . . . This is faithfulness to God's cause. The breastplate gets a coat of "righteousness" in character and conduct . . . This makes you a good person. Spread a little "peace" on your shoes.

PROP CLOWN: Peace? For going into *battle?*

NARRATOR: Of course, peace. Peace, after all, is the reason for doing battle. The shield you'll seal with "faith" . . . in which the worst, most fiery temptations will burn themselves out! You must accept God's "salvation" to seal your helmet *(PROP CLOWN*

87

seals it and places it on WEARER's head) ... **This gives you protection. And his "Word" will seal your sword.** *(Seals it and hands it over.)* ... **This makes the sword sharp.**

Before you go into battle, there is one more thing you'll need. *(CLOWNS reject the idea of more stuff — he's already overloaded!)* **You'll need an open line of communication with your superior.** *(PROP CLOWN gets out walkie-talkies.)* **No, no, no! Roman soldiers didn't have walkie-talkies! They had messengers. But the Christian soldier has an even better system. Prayer — open communication with God.** *(CLOWNS do "whew!" again.)*

(To WEARER) **Now, why are you all dressed up like this?**

PROP CLOWN: Because his New Year's resolution is Ephesians 6:11 — "Put on the whole armor of God, that ye may be able to stand against the wiles of the devil." (KJV)

NARRATOR: That's a good resolution for all of us. Let's say it together — "Put on the whole armor of God that ye may be able to stand against the wiles of the devil."

(Finish by moving into the audience — WEARER bumbles, trying to maneuver all his equipment.)

The Legend of Befana

by Janet Litherland

Many people believe that the wise men arrived at the stable in Bethlehem with the shepherds, because that is how tradition has portrayed the nativity scene. Actually, they arrived later, and the time of their coming is called "Epiphany," which celebrates the manifestation, or appearance, of God on earth. The following legend, about being too busy for the Messiah, is popular in Italy, Russia, and other countries.

CAST: Three MALE CLOWNS, one FEMALE CLOWN, NARRATOR.

PROPS: Container of candies wrapped in gold foil, sock filled with talcum powder, spray can of air freshener, three roses — one up sleeve of each male clown, broom, feather duster, pot of water, dipper, three chairs, lantern, shawl.

SETTING: NARRATOR is at lectern at side of stage. Chairs are randomly arranged On-stage. Broom leans against back wall next to lantern. Shawl is draped over one of the chairs. WOMAN CLOWN is dusting chairs with feather duster.

OPENING: MALE CLOWNS dressed as wise men and carrying "gifts" (candies, sock, spray can) enter from back, moving slowly toward stage. All CLOWNS are silent and pantomime the story as NARRATOR reads. NARRATOR pauses, as appropriate, to accommodate the action.

NARRATOR: Once upon a time, because all good stories start that way, three wise men were following a big, bright star that would eventually lead them to Bethlehem. They wanted to meet another King — a Baby, who had been born "King of the Jews." And they wanted to give him wonderful gifts.

First in line was Melchior, King of Arabia. In his hand was a pot of gold. *(MELCHIOR holds pot high, showing it to audience, then he unwraps a piece of* *"gold" — candy — and eats it! He continues to eat, occasionally, during the play.)* **This was the best gift he could think of to honor the Baby.**

Next came Caspar, King of Tarsus. He was carrying frankincense to use in worshiping the new King. *(CASPAR swings his sock around, tapping it against his arm, "blessing" the audience with the powder that comes out.)*

Last, but certainly not least *(Use tallest CLOWN)*, **came Balthazar, King of Sheba. Balthazar had chosen myrrh as his gift, a perfume used for embalming, because it smelled good. He was sure the Baby would like that!** *(BALTHAZAR sprays tiny wisps of scent over heads of audience.)*

Well, they had been traveling for a long time, and they were tired and thirsty. Lucky for them, they saw a light in a house not far off the path. So they decided to take a little detour and ask for a drink of water and a place to rest.

As it happened, the house belonged to an old woman named Befana, who was very busy cleaning it. When she heard the knock at her door . . . she was so busy that she didn't even want to answer it. But the knocking persisted . . . Finally, she went to the door . . . opened it *(BEFANA pantomimes action)* **. . . and was surprised . . . and awed . . . at the sight of such splendor! Melchior offered her a piece of gold . . . which she immediately ate . . . and another, which she immediately pocketed. Caspar blessed her, which made her sneeze, but she loved it . . . and Balthazar sprayed her with his good-smelling perfume . . . Wow! She was so enthralled that she invited the wonderful personages to enter her humble home.**

Befana tried her best to make them comforta-

ble. *(She scurries to arrange the chairs — use bumbling, fall-down slapstick here to make it funny.)* ... **Finally, when the great, rich rulers were seated, she asked what she could give them to eat ... She hoped, of course, that they didn't want much, because she didn't *have* much!** *(She indicates this to audience.)* **... "Only a drink of water," Melchior said, and the others agreed ... Befana was greatly relieved ... and ran to get the pot and dipper.** *(Goes Off-stage.)* **In no time at all she was back, being very accommodating.** *(Runs right back in, slopping water everywhere. If possible, she does a slip-and-fall routine, handing the pot to one of the kings just before she loses it.)*

While the great kings refreshed themselves, Befana grabbed her broom and began to sweep ... She still had a lot of cleaning to do before nightfall, and she *always* finished whatever she started. She managed to sneak a few glances at the kings while she worked ... because they were so, well, *kingly!* ... She even maneuvered her broom around their chairs so she could feel the richness of the fabrics they wore. *(Use lots of clown business here.)*

Finally, the kings stood ... saying that they must leave, that they had a long way to go ... "Where are you going?" asked Befana ... And they told her about the Baby King who had been born in Bethlehem, the "King of the Jews."

"We're taking him gifts," Melchior said, eating a piece of his gold ... "We're going to worship him," Caspar said, socking the frankincense against his arm, which made Befana sneeze, but she loved it ... "And we're gong to make him smell good," added Balthazar, spraying Befana with his lovely myrrh, which made Befana sneeze again, but she

91

loved it . . . Wow!

"Wait!" she cried, grabbing her broom in one hand and her duster in the other. She thought that if these fabulous personages were taking gifts to yet another king, that new King must really be *something!* "Wait until I finish cleaning my house and I'll go with you!" . . . And she began to clean with the speed and fury of a flying camel . . .

But they rose *(WISE MEN each pull rose out of sleeve and hand to BEFANA)* . . . saying they couldn't wait. They were very sorry . . . But they did invite her to come along when the cleaning was done . . . They pointed to the star . . . and showed her the path to follow . . . She did stop long enough to wave good-bye . . . as they left in one accord. That means in agreement, not in a Honda. *(WISE MEN exit through the audience, as they came — eating, blessing, and spraying. NARRATOR continues.)*

So Befana continued cleaning . . . *(Dusts, sweeps, and rearranges chairs.)* By the time she finished, it was dark outside . . . *(Looks out.)* Nevertheless, she was determined to see the Baby King. She grabbed her trusty lantern . . . wrapped a shawl around her shoulders . . . and started out. *(She exits down center aisle, the way of the WISE MEN — be sure they are out of sight. She moves quickly to the back of the room, out of sight.)*

Trouble is, when she finally arrived at the stable, she was far too late. Mary, Joseph, and the Baby were gone. So were the shepherds and the angels. What she found were people who told her what a spectacular event she'd missed, the coming of the Messiah!

(BEFANA comes back down the aisle, looking at individual

members of audience. She is frustrated and confused.)

From that day to this, Befana has wandered the earth . . . looking for the Baby . . . the Messiah . . . the one she had missed. She'd had a *golden* opportunity *(Pulls gold-wrapped candy from pocket and shows it to audience)* **to come face-to-face with the Messiah . . . but she threw it away** *(Tosses candy to someone in audience)* **. . . all because she'd been *too busy!*** *(BEFANA exits through a side door near, but not on, the stage.)*

NARRATOR'S ROUND OFF: And now, to take three Scriptures out of context and mix them unmercifully: "While thy servant was busy here and there, he was gone. There is a time for every purpose and for every work. It is time to seek the Lord!" (I Kings 20:40, Ecclesiastes 3:17, Hosea 10:12, KJV)

NATIONAL NOTHING DAY
(or any other day)

To Him Who Does Nothing, Will Nothing Be Given

by Janet Litherland

CAST: A troupe of CLOWNS (Two or more can double the parts, but the more the better!), a MINISTER.

PROPS: Each clown has his or her own specialty props — puppet, balls, balloons, magic tricks, etc.

SETTING: Stage is full of lazy CLOWNS sitting, standing, and lying down in different positions doing absolutely nothing (arrange an interesting picture).

OPENING: At first they don't talk — just move slightly, shifting positions. They look at one another. One waves at the audience. One yawns; one snores. (Create a funny scene with limited action.)

CLOWN 1:   **Man, this is great! A whole day of doing nothing!** *(CLOWNS react, "Yeah, wonderful!" etc.)*

MINISTER: *(Enters, stepping over CLOWNS to Center Stage.)* **What in the world is *this*?**

CLOWN 2:   **It's National Nothing Day. We're doing nothing, and it's great!**

MINISTER: **I see. And who will deliver the "Meals on Wheels" today?**

CLOWN 3:   **Someone else.**

MINISTER: **Who will collect clothing for the poor?**

CLOWN 4:   **Someone else.**

MINISTER: **I guess the "someone" is me. I must say, I'm disappointed in you.** *(Exits.)*

CLOWN 5:   *(Calls after him.)* **Lighten up, Reverend. It's a holiday!**

(CLOWNS, one at a time, begin doing their specialty acts until all are finally going at once. It's a spectacular scene,

almost like a circus, and they're having a wonderful time! Let it go on long enough for the audience to really enjoy it. Play background music. But then . . . the MINISTER returns.)

MINISTER: **Excuse me!** *(Action stops.)* **Aren't you supposed to be doing *nothing?***

CLOWN 6: **We're just doing our "thing" — that's nothing.**

MINISTER: **I don't agree. If National Nothing Day means you do nothing, then you do *nothing*, not even your "thing"!** *(CLOWNS groan and put away their toys, taking their former positions.)*

CLOWN 7: **If we can't do our thing, what *can* we do?**

MINISTER: **Nothing. That's the whole idea, isn't it? Well, I'll be on my way.** *(Starts to exit.)*

CLOWN 8: **Hey, Reverend! Would you bring back some sandwiches? We're getting hungry.** *(CLOWNS agree.)*

MINISTER: **Sorry, I've got to deliver "Meals on Wheels" to people who are *really* hungry.**

CLOWN 9: *(Mumbles, but so all can hear.)* **I'm beginning to wonder if this "nothing" business is all it's cracked up to be.**

CLOWN 8: **But Reverend, how are we supposed to eat? We can't get it ourselves.**

MINISTER: *(Speaks as if quoting.)* **To him who does nothing, will nothing be given.**

CLOWN 9: *(Rises.)* **I don't know about the rest of you, but I've had enough of this.** *(Exits. He is followed by others, one at a time, with lines like "Me too," "I'm hungry," "I'm getting bored," "I want to go home," etc. Only one clown remains.)*

CLOWN 10: *(To MINISTER)* **Need some help with "Meals on Wheels"?**

MINISTER: *(Smiles.)* **I sure do.**

CLOWN 10:   *(Quotes as he starts off.)* **"To him who does nothing, will nothing be given." That's some powerful Bible verse, Reverend.** *(Exits.)*

MINISTER: *(To audience)* **I never said it was in the Bible . . . but maybe it ought to be!** *(Exits in same direction as CLOWN 10.)*

Mine!

by Tommy Thomson
(Clownbo)

CAST: CLOWN, NARRATOR.

PROPS: Bag of sweets (candy), small balloon, small hand pump.

MIME SKETCH: Clown enters. Smiles at audience. Produces a bag of sweets from his pocket, opens bag, smiles again, then puts hand into bag and pulls out a sweet. Clown holds this sweet up and makes drooling faces at it, licking lips, etc. Then clown puts sweet in his mouth and chews it, with a happy and contented look on his face. As he chews, he uses hand pump to blow up balloon hidden under his clothing.

Clown looks at audience and holds out open bag to them, as if to say, "Do you want one?" as a child might do. Then he quickly draws his hand back and pops another couple of sweets into his own mouth, pointing to himself and miming, "They're mine!" As he chews, he pumps the balloon a bit more.

Clown pops another couple of sweets in mouth and chews, then another, and another — each time pumping balloon a bit more — until the balloon bursts. Clown falls to ground, miming death.

NARRATOR: And Jesus said, "Watch out! Be on your guard against all kinds of greed; a man's life does not consist in the abundance of his possessions." (Luke 12:15, NIV)

NOTE FROM TOMMY: I usually round off with some words like, "Lots of things that appear good to us

are often bad for us. But the fact that they look good to us is temptation. Only God is truly good. If we learn about him through Christ, we learn to follow and serve; we learn to give of our gifts — our possessions, ourselves — to others, and are richly blessed as we lift others up in our giving before God." *(During these words, CLOWN hands out remaining sweets to members of the audience.)*

TOMMY'S SAFETY NOTE: Wear an extra T-shirt below the outer one, as it is not a good idea to burst the balloon, no matter how small, next to bare skin. It leaves some redness. I also tape the mouth of the balloon to the mouth of the pump.

In Due Season

Based on Ecclesiastes 3:1-8

by Janet Litherland

CAST: One CLOWN, one little GIRL.

PROPS: Piece of cardboard (about 2' x 3') folded to stand alone on floor, big clown sunglasses, parasol, beach bag with towel and sandwich.

SETTING: A paper "hole" is taped to floor, center; sign nearby says, "Groundhog Hole."

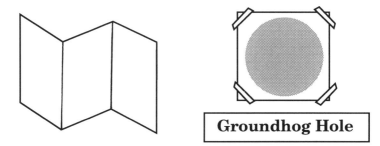

Groundhog Hole

(CLOWN enters on tiptoe carrying all props. Sneaks up to hole and quietly places props on floor nearby. Tiptoes around hole, tries to peek in — involves audience in this play. He/she is going to try to prevent the groundhog from seeing his shadow: Looks for direction of sun, "measures" the angle, sets up cardboard wall, measures again, adjusts wall — keeps peeking into hole and playing with audience to "shh." Finally satisfied, he sits behind wall where he can keep an eye on hole. Tries on sunglasses and removes them, shakes out towel, admires it, and folds it lovingly, sets up parasol, stretches out under it, then sits up and closes it — he is anticipating a day at the beach. After another peek into the hole, he takes out sandwich and begins to eat.)

GIRL: *(Enters.)* **Hi, Clownie!** *(Use CLOWN's real name.)* **What are you doing?**

CLOWN: **Shhh! Come here. I'm waiting for the groundhog to come out.**

GIRL: *(Moves toward CLOWN.)* **So he can see his shadow?**

CLOWN: **Ha! I've fixed it so he** *can't* **see his shadow. See?** *(Indicates the wall.)* **I've put this between him and where his shadow would be!**

GIRL: **Why?**

CLOWN: *(Stands.)* **Because, if he sees his shadow, he'll go right back inside and we'll have six more weeks of winter. I want to go to the** *beach.* **I've got everything ready!**

GIRL: **Clownie, the groundhog doesn't control the seasons — God does.**

CLOWN: **God? Oh, yeah — "To everything there is a season, a time for this and a time for that."** *(GIRL nods.)* **You mean even if I fix it so the groundhog can't see his shadow, and God wants it to be winter, it will still be winter?**

GIRL: **That's right.** *(CLOWN thinks a minute, then quickly gathers up his stuff.)* **Now what are you doing?**

CLOWN: **If God is in charge, there's only one way to talk with him and that's to pray. I'm going right home and get down on my knees and pray for summer!**

GIRL: **Why are you hurrying?**

CLOWN: **I have to get it done before the groundhog sees his shadow!** *(Exits.)*

GIRL: *(Laughs, then speaks to audience.)* **He doesn't have to go home to talk with God. God is everywhere. If Clownie** *really* **wanted to hurry, he'd get down on his knees** *right here.* *(Points. CLOWN comes running back in, sunglasses on, plops to his knees beside "hole,"* *and begins to pray. GIRL to audience)* **It may not do any good if God's mind is made up, but at least Clownie understands now.**

A Party Walkaround

by Janet Litherland

SINGING TELEGRAMS

Clown wears a sign on his/her back, "I deliver singing telegrams, just ask!" When approached, he has the sender point out the person to receive the message and asks what the message is *(Only "nice" ones!)*. Clown then takes a roll of masking tape from pocket and has customer sign on end of roll. Puts roll back in pocket.

Clown approaches the lucky receiver, explains that he has a message to deliver, then sings it. *(Use a funny voice and whatever clown props or giveaways normally carried that may be appropriate: A puppet, paper hearts, heart-shaped cookies, love balloons, etc.)*

When message is finished, Clown tells the person that he's made a "tape" so that the moment may be remembered forever. Takes out roll, tears off the sender's signature, and sticks it on the receiver.

VALENTINE'S DAY
A Gift of Love

by Janet Litherland

CAST: FEMALE CLOWN with lots of pocket space, MALE CLOWN.

PROPS: A "Chunky" brand candy bar in pocket of male clown, bag of candy bars as specified in script — they are fastened together with tiny pieces of tape, just enough to keep them in order until they are removed from bag one at a time.

OPENING: FEMALE rushes On-stage and begins speaking to audience.

FEMALE: **Hi! Happy Valentine's Day! Guess what?! My boyfriend will be along in a minute and he has a Valentine present for me — he said so! I know what that means — candy! But not just any old candy. Valentine candy comes in a big red heart all decorated with flowers and lace, and it says "I love you" on it. Boy, that really makes a girl feel special. And I love candy, too — all kinds. Those heart-shaped boxes have some of everything — caramels, nuts, creams — oh, I can hardly wait! I never had a Valentine present before. Course I never had a boyfriend who really loved me before, either. At least I *think* he does. I *hope* he does! But if he's bringing me a beautiful red heart full of Valentine candy, he surely *must* love me! . . . Oh, here he comes!**

MALE: *(Enters, holding bag of candy bars behind back.)* **Hi, sweetie!** *(FEMALE giggles.)* **Happy Valentine's Day.** *(FEMALE giggles again and MALE speaks in "sing-song" voice.)* **I brought you something.**

FEMALE: *("Sing-songs" back.)* **I know.**

MALE: **You know I've never been too good with words.**

FEMALE: *(Coyly)* **I know.**

103

MALE: So this present will say what's in my heart. *(FEMALE giggles and mouths "I told you so" to audience. MALE brings bag around front and hands it to FEMALE.)* **Here!** *(Now he turns his joyfully expectant face to audience.)*

FEMALE: *(Looks inside and is crestfallen.)* **A bag of candy bars!**

MALE: Yep.

FEMALE: But where's . . . I thought . . . *(Almost in tears)* This says what's on your *heart?*

MALE: Yep. Let me show you. *(Takes bag back and begins removing bars, one at a time. He holds each one up at the appropriate place in his speech.)*

(As each bar is named, MALE shows it to audience, then puts it in one of FEMALE's many pockets. As his tale unfolds, FEMALE brightens, is pleased, then delighted. MALE speaks with exaggerated feeling. NOTE: If some of the following bars are not available in your area, substitute others and change the words to fit.)

MALE: When I met you, my heart went *Crunch*, and my legs turned to *Butterfingers*. My head was a *Starburst* of wonder, and in my ears I heard a *Symphony* of joy. It was better than *Pay Day!* I knew that not across *Mounds* of earth, up the *Milky Way*, or even over to *Mars*, would I find a more wonderful woman, *Bar None*. So now I'm going to *Zero* in. If you will be my *Bit-O-Honey*, I will be your *Mr. Big*. And there'll be plenty of *Kisses* for *Now and Later!*

FEMALE: Oh, _____! *(CLOWN's name) (To audience)* **Who needs a heart-shaped box anyway?** *(To MALE)* **You *really* do know how to make a girl feel special!** *(Takes his arm, giggling, and they start to walk off. As they go, MALE pulls one last candy bar from his pocket and says to audience, aside:)*

MALE: I sure hope all this candy doesn't make her Chunky! *(Tosses "Chunky" candy bar into audience as they exit.)*

Mining for Gold

Based on I Corinthians 13

by Mark Seckel
(Marko)

AUTHOR'S NOTE: This is not necessarily a Valentine's Day skit, but it is about love, the best love of all, and it's definitely appropriate for Valentine's Day as well as any other day.

CAST: One CLOWN.

PROPS: Large box labeled "Sonshine Mine," hard hat, digging equipment, three small foam rocks labeled "money," "fame," and "things owned," large foam rock painted gold and labeled "love," wheelbarrow, catalog labeled "Heavenly General Store Trade Book."

PREPARATION: Place the "Sonshine Mine" Center Stage with rocks inside it. Place digging equipment and book in wheelbarrow Off-stage.

CLOWN: *(Enters whistling, wearing hat, pushing wheelbarrow.)* **Guess what? I was just given the deed to this mine. That means I own it! Can you imagine? Some guy just gave it to me! Wow! What a day. Let's see ... yep, this is it, the "Sonshine Mine." I'll just dig out some valuable minerals and be rich in no time at all. Just think of it. I won't have to worry about working ever again!** *(Makes mine-digging sounds — hammer, musical triangle.)*

   Ouch! What's this? *(Brings out rock labeled "money.")* **Wow! This must be worth a lot! I'll just look in my catalog and see what this is worth.** *(Thumbs through catalog)* **Ah! Here it is, money ... Let's see ... "Money is used to buy things we need to live on every day, like food, clothing, and houses. Some people love money for what it will buy them, and soon forget important things like**

friends and helping others . . . Value, two cents." What? This is only worth two cents! *(Puzzled)* Well, let me try again. *(Throws rock aside.)*

Hmmm, I wonder what this is. *(Brings out rock labeled "fame.")* **Oh boy!** This must be worth something. *(Looks in catalog again.)* Here it is . . . fame . . . "Being known by many people. Some people are famous for good reasons, but too many people are famous for being unkind, cruel, or very selfish . . . Value, two cents." What? According to the catalog, this is only worth two cents! This is disappointing. Let's try again.

(Pulls out rock labeled "things owned.") **Wow!** Look at this. Certainly this must be worth something. *(Thumbs through catalog.)* . . . Things owned. "People sometimes value their possessions so much that they don't share them with others and therefore do not gain the satisfaction of helping others enjoy life . . . Value, two cents." Wow, this is ridiculous! No wonder that guy gave this mine to me. There's nothing in it. Let me try again.

(Makes big noise, as if huge rock fell on him.) **Ouch!** What in the world is this? *(Pulls out rock labeled "love.")* Hmmm . . . I wonder if this rock has any value. *(Consults catalog.)* Yes, here it is . . . love. "The most important thing in the universe. Love helps people work together, it helps solve many problems, and. . . . God made the universe with love. Value? Too great to mention! If you have love, you are rich! *(CLOWN jumps up and down.)*

I'm rich! I'm rich! *(To audience)* This mine really was worth something. I think I'll share this with all the people I can. *(Puts rock in wheelbarrow and exits whistling.)*

Free Love

by Pam Akin for Gracie & E. T. C.

CAST: Two CLOWNS.

PROPS: Four cards big enough for audience to see (about 12" x 18") with LOVE written on each one. Three of the cards are decorated fancy with colors and sparkles; the fourth is plain. Each of the three decorated cards has a string (about 36" long) attached; at the end of each string is another card with one of the following messages. Card one: You must have lots of money. Card two: You must wear the right clothes. Card three: You can never do anything wrong.

Also, box in which to put the four cards, sign that says "Free Love," a TV tray or small table.

CLOWN 1:   *(Enters and makes a big production of carrying in a box of love. After he has set the box on the table, he shows audience the "Free Love" sign.)* **Step right up! Step right up! I'm giving out free love today.**

CLOWN 2:   *(Slowly approaches CLOWN 1.)* **I could use some love.**

CLOWN 1:   **Well, then, you have come to the right place. Just look in my box, pull out the love you want, and it's yours!**

CLOWN 2:   *(After looking in box, pulls out a LOVE, not noticing the string attached.)* **Oh, I like this one!** *(Shows it to audience.)*

CLOWN 1:   That's a mighty fine choice. Oops! There is a **string attached!** *(CLOWN 1 follows the string and notices there is a card attached.)* **Hey, it says something. "You must have lots of money." Do you have lots of money?** *(CLOWN 2 sadly shakes head and turns pockets inside out.)* **Well, I'm sorry, but in order to have this LOVE you have to have lots of money. But don't worry, I have more love. Look in my box and pick out another.**

CLOWN 2:   I like this one. It's really nice. I could use this love.

CLOWN 1:   Then it's yours. *(Pause)* **Wait a minute. There is a string attached.** *(CLOWN 1 follows the string and reads the card.)* **"You must wear nice clothes."** **Hmmm . . .** *(He looks CLOWN 2 up and down.)* **Are those nice clothes?**

CLOWN 2:   I think so. I like them.

CLOWN 1:   Turn around for me and let me take a better look. *(CLOWN 2 turns around.)* **They're OK, but not nearly nice enough for this LOVE. Pick out another one.**

CLOWN 2:   *(Looks in box and pulls out the prettiest LOVE yet.)* **Oh, this is beautiful! It's the prettiest love I have ever seen! Surely I can have this one! Oh, no! There's another string attached!**

CLOWN 1:   *(After once again following the string to the card)* **Here's what it says: "You must never do anything wrong." Uh, oh, that's a hard one. Do you ever do anything wrong?** *(CLOWN 2 shakes head no with conviction.)* **Are you sure? I think it is very hard not to do anything wrong. You have never done *anything* wrong?**

CLOWN 2:   *(Is very sad)* **I have done things wrong. Does this mean I can't have this very beautiful LOVE?**

CLOWN 1:   I'm afraid that's what it means. But I have

one more LOVE. *(Reaches into box and takes out last, simple LOVE.)* **It's not the most attractive to the eyes, but it does not have a string. Do you want it?** *(Hands it to CLOWN 2.)*

CLOWN 2:   *(Takes the plain LOVE.)* **You're right. It is not the prettiest love you have. Why doesn't it have a string attached?**

CLOWN 1:   **That is God's love, and God's love doesn't have strings attached. God gives his love freely. He doesn't care if you have lots of money or are poor. He doesn't care if you wear pretty clothes or must wear rags. And even though he hopes you try very hard not to do anything wrong, he still offers his love and forgiveness when you mess up. All he wants in return is for us to love him, too. Actually, his simple love has turned out to be the most beautiful love I can offer you today. Do you want it?**

CLOWN 2:   **Oh, yes! Yes, I do!**

CLOWN 1:   **Then it is yours. But don't keep it to yourself — share God's love with others as I have shared it with you.**

PRESIDENTS' DAY

A Good Leader

by Janet Litherland

CAST: Two clowns — JOEY and BONE. (BONE must have good slapstick skills, pratfalls, etc.)

PROPS: Big clown watch for JOEY, coat for BONE.

SETTING: Sign on back wall — "Joey's Exercise Class."

OPENING: JOEY is pacing floor, looking at his watch.

BONE: *(Enters hurriedly.)* **Hi! Sorry I'm late.** *(Looks around.)* **Where is everybody?**

JOEY: **That's what I'd like to know. Class should have started ten minutes ago.**

BONE: *(Takes off coat and throws it aside on floor.)* **Maybe they're not coming because of the holiday.**

JOEY: **What holiday?**

BONE: **Today is Presidents' Day.**

JOEY: **What does that mean?**

BONE: **It means the banks are closed.**

JOEY: **No, what does it *really* mean?**

BONE: **It honors our Presidents, especially George Washington and Abraham Lincoln, because their birthdays are this month.**

JOEY: **My birthday's this month, too.**

BONE: **Yeah? When?**

JOEY: **Day after tomorrow.**

BONE: **Gee, Joey, maybe you'll be President one day! You're a good leader. And that's what Presidents' Day is really all about — leadership.**

JOEY: *(Looks at his watch once more.)* **Well, let's get started. I guess no one else is coming.**

(They begin exercising. JOEY is agile and coordinated — BONE is anything but! Use imagination and develop the

111

routine to suit the talents of participating clowns.)

JOEY: **We'll start with warm-up stretches. Right . . .** *(He stretches right, arm overhead.)* **Left . . .** *(Same to left. BONE goes right just fine, but when he stretches left, he goes all the way over, onto the floor. JOEY helps him up.)*

BONE: **Sorry, Joey. You know I'm not very good at this.**

JOEY: **That's OK, Bone. That's why you're here. Let's try some leg kicks. Right . . . left . . . right . . . left . . .** *(BONE does the first few, but then his legs go out from under him and he lands on his buttocks.)*

(That's the idea. Continue with several exercises, including leg lifts that end in a back somersault for BONE, cat stretches for the back — BONE's arms give out and he lands on his stomach, etc. JOEY is always kind and helpful. When session is over, BONE hurts all over and can hardly walk.)

BONE: **That sure was a workout! I don't know why I keep coming back. I can't figure out if you're being good to me or trying to kill me!**

JOEY: *(Laughs.)* **You're doing fine, Bone. What counts is that you're physically fit.**

BONE: **You're kidding, right?**

JOEY: **No. You've got your heart rate up and your muscles are active. You're in good shape, Bone.**

BONE: **So are you, Joey. You should belong to the President's Council on Physical Fitness!** *(BONE gives JOEY a good-natured slap, and this time JOEY goes sprawling across floor.)* **Whoops! Sorry! Oh, gosh, I'm sorry!** *(Helps JOEY up.)*

JOEY: **That's OK, Bone. You're a good student.**

BONE: **And you're a good leader, Joey. You're patient and kind, and super smart.** *(Starts to exit.)* **See you next week. Oh, by the way — Happy Birthday day after tomorrow, and Happy Presidents' Day!** *(Exits*

while talking to himself.) **Yep, Joey's a real good leader!**
JOEY: *(Happily and proudly to audience)* **Gee, maybe I
ought to run for President!** *(Exits.)*

Right Now, God?

by Janet Litherland

CAST: One CLOWN, VOICE OF GOD (Off-stage), an audience "plant."

PROPS: Juggling balls or balloons, fishing pole with big paper hook.

SETTING: A chair, and a few other items that CLOWN can "hide" behind; big box Up Center containing props.

OPENING: CLOWN enters and selects balls or balloons from prop box (whatever he/she does best) then sits and begins working with them. When VOICE OF GOD speaks, CLOWN reacts in big way — yells, and balls go everywhere or balloons pop.

VOICE OF GOD: Good morning, Clownie. *(Use CLOWN's name.)*

CLOWN: *(Reacts.)* **What was that? What was that?!**

VOICE: This is God, Clownie.

CLOWN: Yeow! *(Runs behind a set prop and "hides.")*

VOICE: Don't be afraid. I just want to talk with you. You're not at work today.

CLOWN: I — I'll go tomorrow, I promise! *(Looks around for a better place to hide and sneaks to a chair.)*

VOICE: You can't hide from me, Clownie.

CLOWN: *(Pokes head under chair and speaks straight out to audience.)* **I can try!**

VOICE: I have a job for you. Are you interested?

CLOWN: *(To audience)* **Not really.**

VOICE: What was that, Clownie? Did you say something?

CLOWN: Uh ... why me, God? Why *me?*

VOICE: Ah, Clownie, you're the best I've got. Now come out from under that chair.

CLOWN: How about later, God? *(To audience)* **After he**

goes away!

VOICE: How about now, Clownie? . . . And I don't go away. *(CLOWN claps hand over mouth, then wriggles out and stands at attention in front of chair.)* **The job I have in mind is a difficult one.**

CLOWN: *(Groans, then starts to rattle off excuses.)* **I already have a job, a nice home, good friends, I like the town I live in, I'm real busy —**

VOICE: Sit on it!

CLOWN: *(Instantly drops onto the chair.)* Uh — ha, ha, God. You have a sense of humor.

VOICE: And I'm losing it along with my patience. Clownie, I want you to be a fisher of men.

CLOWN: I already am a fisherman. That's my job. *(To audience)* He should know that.

VOICE: Not fisherman — fisher of men. *People,* Clownie.

CLOWN: You want me to fish for *people?* Ugh! Excuse me, God, but that's gross! They'd get the hook stuck in them and they'd really be mad! Let me show you. *(Runs to prop box.)* This will just take a minute. *(Pulls out pole with big colorful paper hook. Winds up and casts it into audience, where "plant" jumps up and yells, "Oow!")*

VOICE: No, no, no, Clownie! You're not going to hurt people — you're going to save them.

CLOWN: Save them? From what?

VOICE: From their sins, so they can follow me, which is what I want you to do.

CLOWN: *(Wails.)* But I can't even see you!

VOICE: You can hear me, can't you? *(No answer)* *Clownie?*

CLOWN: *(Jumps.)* Yes! I hear you very well!

VOICE: So — put away your toys and take up your new job. I'm going to help you with it.

CLOWN: *(Suddenly realizes that this is for real. It is an honor, not a burden. Speaks to audience.)* **He really isn't kidding. God wants *me* to work for him — he's going**

to help me with the job. Imagine that! . . . Me! . . . Uh, God?

VOICE: Yes?

CLOWN: Can I start the first of next week?

VOICE: Now, Clownie. It's now or never.

CLOWN: *(Gulps.)* **I'm coming, God.** *(But he doodles around — puts pole away, juggles, or does balloons until VOICE calls.)*

VOICE: *(Loudly)* **Now, Clownie!**

CLOWN: *(Yelps and runs off.)* **I'm coming, I'm coming, I'm coming!**

The Sunday School Lesson

by Janet Litherland

CAST: Two CLOWNS.

PROPS: Big clown book titled "Irish," Bible, big green paper shamrock on Clown 1's costume.

OPENING: CLOWN 1 enters from left, reading book; CLOWN 2 enters from right.

CLOWN 2:   Hi! What are you reading?

CLOWN 1:   I'm studying about the Irish. I have to teach Sunday school next week and, since it will be near St. Patrick's Day, I'd like to teach something about that saint.

CLOWN 2:   What have you learned?

CLOWN 1:   Well, I found out that the Irish love St. Patrick for his faith in God. I also learned that part of the celebration of St. Patrick's Day is to thank God for his care through hundreds of years of sadness.

CLOWN 2:   OK, but for a Sunday school lesson you need to find something really interesting about St. Patrick — something unique.

CLOWN 1:   Hmmm. *(Consults book.)* **. . . How about this? "St. Patrick drove all the snakes out of Ireland by preaching a blistering sermon from a hilltop, accompanied by the sound of a drum. To this day, there isn't one snake in all of Ireland."**

CLOWN 2:   That's good! You could preach a sermon like that and compare the snakes to Satan.

CLOWN 1:   How would I do that?

CLOWN 2:   I have a Bible, let's see . . . *(Opens Bible.)* **OK, I'll read a few snake verses and you beat the drum.**

CLOWN 1:   I don't have a drum.

CLOWN 2:   So clap your hands. *(Begins reading, and*

117

CLOWN 1 begins clapping.) **Genesis 3:14 — "And the Lord God said to the snake, 'Because you tricked the woman into eating the fruit, you, of all the animals, will be punished. From now on you will crawl on your belly and eat dirt!'"** ... Boy! I'll bet that scared a few snakes! *(Reads.)* **Isaiah 27:1 — "On the day the Lord comes down from heaven he will use his powerful sword to punish the wriggling, crooked snake."** ... Wow! He means business! *(Reads.)* **Revelation 20:2-3 — "And he grabbed hold of that old snake, which is Satan, and locked him up for a thousand years so that he could not deceive people any more until his thousand years were up."** *(Author's paraphrase)* ... Ooooh! That one really compares the snake to Satan!

CLOWN 1: Those verses are OK, but they're kind of spooky for Sunday school. I'd rather teach something, well ... nice.

CLOWN 2: What about that shamrock you're wearing? Is there a lesson in that?

CLOWN 1: I don't know. Let's see ... *(Flips pages in his book.)* It's the national emblem of Ireland ... Oh, yeah! It says here that St. Patrick used the shamrock to illustrate the Trinity. He said that the three leaves represent the Father, the Son, and the Holy Spirit — all separate, yet one; and it's the stem — the Godhead — that connects them and makes them one.

CLOWN 2: That's pretty good!

CLOWN 1: That's what I'll teach. That's a good St. Patrick's Day lesson. Hey, thanks for the help! *(Closes his book and starts to exit.)*

CLOWN 2: Uh, say — could I have your shamrock? Please?

CLOWN 1: Sure. *(Takes it off and hands it over.)* **I have**

more at home. Bye! *(Exits.)*

CLOWN 1: *(Admires shamrock.)* **Gee! I couldn't admit it to him, but I never was able to figure out how three separate beings — Father, Son, and Holy Spirit — could still be just *one*. This shamrock makes it real clear to me. I'm going to go home and hang this up in my bedroom!** *(Starts to exit.)* **And I'm glad he didn't decide on the snakes. Those things give me nightmares!** *(Exits.)*

SHROVE TUESDAY

A Flipping Good Time

by Janet Litherland

CAST: Two MALE CLOWNS, one FEMALE CLOWN (Dinah).

PROPS: Two skillets, one pancake — real or fake.

OPENING: CLOWN 1 enters with skillet, flipping pancake and humming. Gets fancy, trying little dance steps and higher flips.

CLOWN 2: *(Enters from other side.)* **Hi! What's going on?**

CLOWN 1: *(Keeps flipping.)* **Today is Shrove Tuesday. Dinah's in the kitchen making pancakes.**

CLOWN 2: **Is someone in the kitchen with Dinah?**

CLOWN 1: **No, why?**

CLOWN 2: **Thought I heard someone strummin' on an old banjo. Hey, let me try that.** *(Reaches for skillet.)*

CLOWN 1: *(Hands skillet to CLOWN 2, who begins flipping, badly.)* **That's Dinah on the banjo. She plays while she cooks. Gettin' ready for the Mardi Gras.**

CLOWN 2: **What's Mardi Gras got to do with Stove Tuesday?** *(Keeps flipping and improving.)*

CLOWN 1: *Shrove!* **It's** *Shrove* **Tuesday. We make pancakes to use up all the milk, eggs, and fat we're not allowed to eat during Lent, which starts tomorrow on Ash Wednesday.**

CLOWN 2: **Smash Wednesday?**

CLOWN 1: *Ash!* **Ash Wednesday — just one of the special days of Lent. There's Good Friday, Palm Sunday, Maundy Thursday . . .**

CLOWN 2: **Monday-Thursday?** *(To audience)* **I think my friend has flipped more than his pancakes!** *(Gives skillet back to CLOWN 1.)* **Here, you take it.**

CLOWN 1: **I've got a better idea — wait!** *(Runs Off-stage*

120

and quickly returns with another skillet.) **I'll flip to you and you catch the pancake in this, then you flip it back to me.**

CLOWN 2:   OK! *(Takes empty skillet and they begin to flip back and forth, skillet to skillet.)* **So what about Mardi Gras?**

CLOWN 1:   That's the last big fling before Lent. We get the merrymaking out of our systems before the "serious" season starts.

CLOWN 2:   How can a clown stop merrymaking?

CLOWN 1:   Actually, we don't. It just takes a different form.

DINAH: *(From Off-stage)* **Clooown! Where are my other skillets? I need them *now!***

CLOWN 2:   Uh-oh, Dinah's quit strummin' on her old banjo.

DINAH: *(Enters, furious.)* **What is this? *Playing* with my skillets? When I'm slaving over a hot stove?**

CLOWN 2:   That's *shrove*, Dinah. *(CLOWN 1 elbows him and they laugh.)*

DINAH: Give me those! *(Grabs both skillets, flips pancake into audience, and starts off.)*

CLOWN 1:   Sorry, Dinah, dear. We were just doing clown things. A skillet isn't only good for cooking, you know. It's also good for a flipping act.

DINAH: *(Ominously)* **Yessss!** *(Turns to them.)* **A skillet is good for many things. And here's one more thing it's good for!** *(Chases CLOWNS off, as if to hit them over their heads.)*

Life's Dust

by Janet Litherland

CAST: TRAMP CLOWN wearing gloves, troupe of MIMES (minimum of three), OFF-STAGE VOICE.

PROPS: Hand puppet, juggling balls, balloon, pin concealed in TRAMP's glove, wand or balancing stick, doughnut, black grease paint stick.

SETTING: Stage is bare except for small stool Down Center and cross on back wall. Except for OFF-STAGE VOICE, this is a silent skit. TRAMP is the persecuted one. MIMES are the persecutors.

MIME SKETCH: **Mimes are Stage Center, "conversing." Tramp enters and tries to join group. They ignore him. He tries to make friends by interesting them in a hand puppet. They turn their backs on him. He moves to other side** (*To face them again*) **and brings out his juggling balls, but as he begins to juggle, they turn again and take several steps in opposite direction.**

   Tramp moves to stool and sits, facing audience. He takes balloon from pocket, inflates it, and begins to create a figure. This catches eye of first mime, who comes up behind him, watching carefully. Mime pulls imaginary ice pick from pocket, checks it for sharpness, letting audience "see" it. When balloon figure is finished and Tramp is admiring it, Mime "sticks" it and it pops. (*Pin is actually employed by TRAMP who has it in his glove.*) **Mime exits and Tramp is sad.**

   Tramp now pulls wand from pocket and balances it in his hand. Second Mime approaches from behind, picks up imaginary ball bat and "shows" it to audience. When wand is balanced nicely, Mime

"bats" it off. *(TRAMP actually does it with a flick of his thumb.)* **Mime exits and Tramp is even more sad.**

Tramp stands, pulls out doughnut and begins eating. Third Mime approaches from behind. He "stomps" on Tramp's toe, and, as Tramp grasps his foot in pain with both hands, the doughnut flies upward. Mime catches the doughnut and exits with it, laughing. Other mimes exit also. Tramp shakes fists at them in anger.

As Tramp sits back down on stool, his anger turns to tears and he begins weeping. Lights dim. Cross on back wall is spotlighted.

Off-stage voice begins reading from Deuteronomy 28. As Scripture is read, Tramp slowly "awakens" to the message, removes his shoes, then rises and goes to cross, kneeling before it, his back to audience.

OFF-STAGE VOICE: **"And it shall come to pass, if thou shalt hearken diligently unto the voice of the Lord thy God, to observe and to do all his commandments which I command thee this day, that the Lord thy God will set thee on high above all nations of the earth:**

"And all these blessings shall come on thee . . . Blessed shalt thou be in the city, and blessed shalt thou be in the field . . . Blessed shalt thou be when thou comest in, and blessed shalt thou be when thou goest out. The Lord shall cause thine enemies that rise up against thee to be smitten before thy face. They shall come out against thee one way, and flee before thee seven ways . . . The Lord shall open unto thee his good treasure, the heaven to give the rain unto thy land in his season, and to bless all the work of thine hand . . .

"And the Lord shall make thee the head, and

**not the tail; and thou shalt be above only, and thou
shalt not be beneath . . . And thou shalt not go aside
from any of the words which I command thee this
day."** (From Deuteronomy 28:1-14, KJV)

*(TRAMP bows his head and, unseen by audience, puts
mark of the cross on his forehead with grease stick.)*

OFF-STAGE VOICE: **"Remember, O Man, that thou art
dust and unto dust shalt thou return."** (Genesis 3:19,
KJV)

*(TRAMP rises and moves Downstage Center, a smile on
his face and a spring in his step. As he picks up his shoes,
MIMES re-enter and cross stage behind him, ignoring him.
He watches them go, blowing kisses to them, then exits in
opposite direction.)*

Sticky Chair

by Rafael Rondon and Carlos Sanchez
(Bombin & Archie)

This skit is our version of the sin box. The idea is not our original. We saw it in a simple way. We liked it, and we made it totally different. Everyone likes this!

CAST: Two CLOWNS (CLOWN A is Auguste or Whiteface, CLOWN B is Tramp or Auguste).

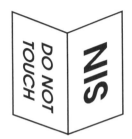

PROPS: Aluminum folding chair (may be painted with bright colors), heavy paper sign (folded, it says "Sin" on one side and "Do Not Touch" on the other.)

OPENING: CLOWN A enters singing or whistling a children's song, such as "Jesus Loves Me." He carries chair in one hand and sign in the other, careful not to show the word "Sin." Continuing his song, he places chair Center Stage, facing audience, then hangs sign over top of chair so that it reads, "Do Not Touch." He looks at the audience, points to sign, then exits.

CLOWN B: *(Enters, passing the chair without notice. A few steps beyond, he stops and thinks, then speaks to audience.)* **I believe I saw a chair!** *(He turns, looking at chair, and reads sign.)* **Do Not Touch!** *(He laughs, then touches* very *fast! Laughs again. Moves to another angle and touches quickly again. Laughs. Now he steps to the left of chair and looks at audience. He boldly removes sign and puts it on floor with "Do Not Touch" showing. Now he grabs chair on top of frame with his right hand. Bending, he looks closely at the chair — under, around, and up, then speaks to audience.)* **There is nothing special about this chair!** *(He decides to leave the room but finds that his right hand is stuck to chair.)* **Oh, no! I'm stuck!**

(Moves around chair without moving hand, picks up chair, may even hit self with it quickly. Now trying to get out, he uses left hand to help, grabbing chair seat with left hand.) **Uh-oh, silly clown, you have stuck your left hand too!**

CLOWN A: *(Begins his song Off-stage but does not enter.)*

CLOWN B: **Somebody's coming!** *(His reaction is to sit on the chair. He puts his right leg between his arms, sitting and "sticking" to the chair. Does not release hands from original positions. He assumes a sad face.)*

CLOWN A: *(Enters, singing. Stops. Speaks to audience.)* **It's my friend!** *(To CLOWN B)* **My friend, what happened?**

CLOWN B: *(Cries and jabbers, gives a few jumps with the chair.)*

CLOWN A: **You mean you're stuck?**

CLOWN B: **Yes!**

CLOWN A: **Don't worry, my friend. I'll help you.** *(Tries to lift CLOWN B from chair by pulling on an arm or leg. He moves the clown, but chair remains "stuck." Chooses another body part and tries again. Fails.)* **OK, I have an idea. We must use our heads!** *(Grabs CLOWN B's head and pulls. Doesn't work. Now he sees sign on floor. Picks it up and reads aloud.)* **"Do Not . . . "** *(Looks at CLOWN B.)* **"Touch."** *(CLOWN B hangs head in shame. CLOWN A now turns sign over.)* **Uh-oh, Sin! . . . I've got a solution for this!** *(Moves to right of CLOWN B, facing away from him. Puts hands in prayer position, closes eyes, and starts praying silently — he moves his mouth like he is talking to God, pointing upward and pointing to CLOWN B.)*

CLOWN B: *(As CLOWN A prays, CLOWN B begins coming "unstuck." Left hand)* **Hey!** *(Right hand)* **Wow!** *(The rest of him)* **Ooooh!** *(CLOWN A continues praying and not looking. CLOWN B moves to stand behind CLOWN A.)*

CLOWN A: **Amen.** *(Looks at the chair expecting to see*

CLOWN B, *but screams, seeing his friend has vanished. Looks to heaven.)* **Ahhh! You got him out!** *(Then looks down, sadly.)* **I wanted to tell him that I love him.**

(CLOWN B now touches CLOWN A's left shoulder. CLOWN A reacts, walking in a circle to see who touched him. CLOWN B follows behind, unseen by CLOWN A. CLOWN B laughs silently.)

CLOWN A: *(Stops and speaks to audience.)* **I wanted to tell him that I was his friend.**

(CLOWN B touches CLOWN A's right shoulder and the circle action is repeated in other direction. This time CLOWN B must end up between CLOWN A and the chair, with CLOWN A looking off to the opposite side.)

CLOWN A: **I wanted to tell him ...** *(Turns abruptly, coming face-to-face with CLOWN B. Both scream with fright, and CLOWN B backs into chair, sitting.)*

CLOWN B: *(Cries.)* **I'm stuck again!**
CLOWN A: **No, no, no, my friend! You can stand now, because he set you free!** *(CLOWN B stands.)* **Let's go and live for him!** *(They exit.)*

Be Persistent

Based on Luke 11:1-13 and adapted from Storytelling From the Bible *by Janet Litherland, copyright © 1991, Meriwether Publishing Ltd.*

by Janet Litherland

CAST: NARRATOR, two CLOWNS, one OLD MAN in a bathrobe.

PROPS: Sandwich, shotgun (or facsimile), a stick-on badge that reads "MARTIN."

SETTING: Door (or curtain opening) Up Center, rural mailbox planted firmly in bucket of sand or stones Center Stage. (MARTIN is printed on it.)

OPENING: CLOWNS are Off Right; OLD MAN is behind door Up Center; NARRATOR is Down Left.

NARRATOR: Many of us have traveled at high noon in the middle of summer in the Deep South. And we have discovered that it's hot! Those of us who don't do well in the stifling heat have learned that it's much better to move through that territory in the cool of evening or even in the dark of night. But there's a problem with that. Unless we stick to the Interstate highways, where the exits have all-night service stations and restaurants, we're not likely to find gasoline, or a hamburger, or anyone to fix a leaky radiator.

Now just suppose you're on your way to Damascus — Damascus, Georgia, that is, down old Route 45 in the middle of the night.

(CLOWNS enter Down Right, propelling themselves along the floor as if they were in a car — driver in front, passenger behind. They pantomime the first part of the story.)

NARRATOR: Your friend in the back seat is real hungry, *(PASSENGER groans loudly and "car" stops, center)* but there aren't any restaurants open. There aren't any restaurants, period. *(Another groan)* But there's a nice little house by the side of the road, and a light is shining from a back window. Someone is awake! *(DRIVER gets out and approaches mailbox, turning it so audience can read MARTIN.)* You look at the mailbox, and lo and behold — the name is Martin, your mother's maiden name. *(DRIVER pulls stick-on badge from pocket and slaps it on his chest.)* Surely these folks, these kinfolks, wouldn't mind fixing your friend a sandwich.

DRIVER: *(Knocks on door. NARRATOR can knock on lectern for sound effect.)*

OLD MAN: *(Speaks gruffly through the door without showing himself. He isn't seen until the end.)* Who's there?

DRIVER: Ummm ... I'm a Martin ... From Pennsylvania?

OLD MAN: You're a long way from home.

DRIVER: I wonder if you could, uh, give me a sandwich. Oh, not for me — it's for my friend. He's real hungry. *(PASSENGER groans.)*

OLD MAN: What are you, some kinda *clown?* Can't you see I'm locked up for the night? My family's asleep ... A sandwich!

DRIVER: Wait! This is real important! *(PASSENGER groans.)*

OLD MAN: Go awaaaaay!

DRIVER: *(Knocks again.)* But you don't understand, sir. We're on our way to Damascus and there aren't any restaurants! My friend really is hungry. *(PASSENGER yelps louder.)*

OLD MAN: A sandwich? That's all? Then you'll go away?

DRIVER: Yes, please ... I'm a Martin, remember? *(Pats his badge to reassure the audience.)*

OLD MAN: Martins lived here before we moved in. Don't like Martins.

DRIVER: *(Slaps his hand over his badge, then rips it off and puts it in his pocket.)* Oh, well, really it's just my mother's maiden name. Pretty far removed, actually.

OLD MAN: Wait.

DRIVER: *(Mouths "Wait?" to the audience. This is his lucky day. He waits on porch, pacing back and forth. PASSENGER groans again.)* You can stop that now. He's getting your sandwich.

PASSENGER: *(Cheerfully)* Okaaay!

DRIVER: *(Runs to "car.")* Hey! I thought your stomach hurt.

PASSENGER: It does, it does! *(Groans again, loudly and pitifully.)*

OLD MAN: Hey, you out there.

DRIVER: *(Runs back onto "porch.")* Yes! Yes, here I am!

OLD MAN: *(Opens door and steps out. He has sandwich in one hand and shotgun in the other.)*

DRIVER: *(Shakes in terror. He tries several times to get the sandwich and avoid the gun — use slapstick techniques — but somehow the gun always ends up in his face. Finally he manages to snatch the sandwich. He backs away toward the car, bowing and thanking as he goes. He hands the sandwich to PASSENGER and says in loud stage whisper:)* You better *share* this one! *(Gets in and they drive Off Left, fast as they can propel themselves.)*

OLD MAN: *(Watches them go, then finally realizes something.)* Wait! *(But they are gone. He turns to audience and says, bewildered:)* That really *was* a clown. *(He exits through his door.)*

NARRATOR: This is one of the stories Jesus told his disciples. Well, sort of. He was teaching them to be persistent in prayer. He finished by saying, "Ask and

you will receive; seek, and you will find; knock, and
the door will be opened to you."

DRIVER: *(From Off-stage)* **Good sandwich!**

PASSENGER: *(From Off-stage, groans loudly.)*

Newspapers for Prayer

by Olive Drane
(Valentine)

CAST: Two or more CLOWNS.

PROPS: Clown's newspaper — 12-16 sheets of a normal newspaper taped together to make a very large paper — folded down to normal size.

SETTING: Bench and a few chairs are Center Stage.

MIME SKETCH: Clowns enter, one carrying folded newspaper. They sit on bench and begin reading paper together. As they read, they comment on various news items, gradually opening out the newspaper. News items would be decided in advance and include a variety of subjects, world and national events, but also include some directly relevant to the audience — local sports achievements, personal honors, etc.

Each time the paper is unfolded, further news items are identified and commented on. Eventually, the clowns will need to stand up on the bench or on chairs to cope with the vast size of the paper. But they do not rush this. They spend time chatting about the various news items.

When the paper becomes too large to handle, it begins to tear. *(A skilled clown might somersault through it.)* **At this point the clowns give up, saying that they have had enough news, and in any case they don't know how to handle this ridiculous newspaper. They gather it up, and wad it into a tight ball, and throw it to someone.** *(Not a clown)* **who is prepared to receive it. This might be the minister or another person, who will then hold it aloft in their**

own hands, and, using the various news items already mentioned by the clowns, make it a focus for congregational prayer.

WORLD DAY OF PRAYER

It's in the Air

Based on Mark 11:24

by Tommy Thomson
(Clownbo)

CAST: One CLOWN, one PARK ATTENDANT.

PROPS: Sign — "Don't Walk on Grass," hats (for clown and park attendant), child's fishing rod, bow and arrow with suction cup, noise of wind.

MIME SKETCH: Clown enters bent over, as if going against a strong wind, holding hat. *(The third fingers of each hand are under hat, ready to flick it upwards.)* **An extra strong gust of wind blows clown's hat off head and off the stage.** *(Clown, using fingers, flicks hat into air. Hat is connected to thread, which is invisible to normal eye, and as hat goes upward, thread is yanked Off-stage, thereby pulling hat out of sight.)*

©MORTON 92 KELWINBRIDGE

Clown starts to run after it but stops abruptly on seeing sign, "Don't Walk on Grass." He turns, motions to audience that hat has blown off, then pulls up shoulders and lifts both arms as if to ask, "What'll I do now?"

Clown looks dejected. Then a look of "I've got an idea" comes over his face. He fetches fishing rod and goes through one or two practice throws. *(Does not actually cast off — have a bit of fun by having hook caught on CLOWN's backside as he practices.)*

Clown casts line out and pulls. Hook is attached to hat. *(This has been quickly done Off-stage.)* **But it's not his hat. Clown looks at it and screws up face into "Won-**

134

der whose it is?"

PARK ATTENDANT: *(Angry)* **Enters, marches to clown, takes hat off him** *(Unhooks it)*, **and scolds him, waving finger. Takes fishing rod and exits in same direction as he entered.**

Clown looks even more dejected. Then there's that look again, "Another bright idea." Clown fetches bow and arrow *(With suction cup and string attached to arrow)*. **He takes aim** *(Toward Off-stage)* **and fires. Clown pulls on string** *(Attached to arrow)*, **and onto stage backs park attendant with suction cup firmly stuck to his backside.** *(He holds suction cup to backside with one or both hands.)*

Park attendant turns to face clown, giving him an angry glare. He pulls off arrow and takes bow from clown. He walks away, but before he gets Off-stage, turns to face clown once more, with a look that says, "Just you try that again, and you're for it!" *(Exits.)*

Clown is really sad. How can he get his hat back? He has another idea. Looks upward, then kneels *(Or sits)* **on ground and prays. While he is praying, a gust of wind blows hat On-stage behind clown** *(To other side of clown from where PARK ATTEN-DANT entered/exited)*.

Clown slowly opens eyes, looks 'round past to where hat blew off, in anticipation, but it isn't there. His slight smile of anticipation turns to a frown. He gets up, shrugs shoulders, and turns to go off *(Opposite side from PARK ATTENDANT)* **and sees hat. Points to it and big broad grin comes over his face. He runs over to hat, picks it up, and puts it on. He is about to walk off, when he remembers what happened in the first place. With a look of "Oh, no, you won't catch me out like that again," to audience, he**

holds onto hat with both hands and exits.

NOTE FROM TOMMY: I usually round this off with a verse of Scripture — "Whatever you ask for in prayer, believe that you have received it, and it will be yours." (Mark 11:24, NIV)

The Hat Shop

by Alan Dragoo and Ellen Griffith
Submitted by David W. Lloyd (Cop a Plea and Poppatui)

CAST: FEMALE CLOWN, MALE CLOWN.

PROPS: Full-length mirror mounted in swivel frame, sign "Hatter," straight-backed chair, hand mirror, fedora, attaché case, costume crown, goblet full of jelly beans, fringed pillow, bishop's miter (enormous, made of construction paper), "gilded" staff, large leather-bound Bible (church altar size), crown of thorns (hanging from altar cross).

OPENING: MALE is seated, FEMALE enters and indicates she wishes to purchase a hat. MALE gestures to indicate he understands. He seats FEMALE and then he exits.

MIME SKETCH: Male enters, walking purposefully and checking his watch, holding fedora and attaché case. He carefully arranges hat on Female's head, and hands her the hand mirror so that she can see how it looks from the rear. She is undecided. He opens attaché case, and attempts to sell her the ensemble. She considers it, but indicates it's not what she's looking for.

Male regretfully removes hat and exits. Female continues to consider herself in the mirror. Male returns, striding with self-importance in a kingly fashion, carrying a crown on pillow and a goblet full of jelly beans. He places crown on Female's head. Her face and manner light up with excitement, then slowly turn to indecision, then to rejection. Male tries to tempt her with the jelly beans, but no sale.

Male regretfully removes crown and exits. Female continues to consider herself in the mirror.

Male returns, marching with a processional step, wearing a bishop's miter and carrying a staff in one hand and a Bible in the other, which he kisses every few steps. He removes miter and places it on Female's head. Her face becomes sober, and she examines herself piously, but rejects it. Male tries to point out the virtues of the Bible, but no sale.

Male becomes visibly discouraged, removes miter and exits. Female continues to consider herself in the mirror. Male returns, indicating he has no more hats in inventory. He tries one more time to interest her in the merchandise, lifting each in turn for her reaction.

Female gets up to leave, then catches sight of crown of thorns on altar cross. She indicates her interest in it, and Male dismisses it. Female goes to cross and removes crown of thorns, places it on her head. Her face goes from neutral to deep sorrow to deep joy with dignity. She leaves, wearing the crown of thorns. Male remains and shrugs his shoulders.

Playing With Temptation

Based on Luke 4:1-13

by Janet Litherland

CAST: Three clowns — WHITEFACE, AUGUSTE, TRAMP.

PROPS: Several stones in pocket of Whiteface and some inflated balloons attached to the back of his belt, stepstool, stepladders, big scripts, hat pin or other sharp object for Tramp.

SETTING: Stage is bare except for stepstool at left and stepladder, right. WHITEFACE is going to direct a play about the temptations of Jesus. (Feel free to add clown "business.")

WHITEFACE: *(Hurries in to center with script and speaks to TRAMP and AUGUSTE who are behind, Off-stage.)* **Come on! Come on! There's only an hour till show time, and you don't know what to do yet!**

(TRAMP and AUGUSTE enter reluctantly, looking around.)

TRAMP: **It's lonely in here.**

WHITEFACE: **Well, it won't be when the audience arrives. I was lucky to find you two. Still can't believe both of my actors got sick at the last minute.**

AUGUSTE: **I can believe it. This place is a dump!**

WHITEFACE: **No, it's not. It's the wilderness.** *(To TRAMP)* **You! Come here and sit on the ground.**

TRAMP: **You mean the floor?**

WHITEFACE: **The *ground*. You're an actor, remember?**

TRAMP: **No, I'm not.**

WHITEFACE: **You are now. Sit!** *(TRAMP moves too slowly, so WHITEFACE whacks him on the shoulder.)* **Hurry!** *(TRAMP's bottom slams to the floor.)* **You're alone in the wilderness and there's nothing to eat.**

139

TRAMP: Who's alone?

WHITEFACE: You are. You're Jesus. Be good!

TRAMP: *(Shocked)* **Me?** ... ***Jesus?*** *(He looks at his clothes, wondering, then becomes pleased with the honor and sits up straight.)*

AUGUSTE: So, who am I, if he's Jesus and he's alone?

WHITEFACE: You're the devil.

AUGUSTE: *(Offended)* **The devil I am!**

WHITEFACE: *(Slaps him on back.)* **Good impersonation! You're here to tempt Jesus.** *(Pulls AUGUSTE to center.)* **You see he's hungry, so you give him these stones and tell him to turn them into bread.** *(Gives stones to AUGUSTE.)*

TRAMP: How about pizza? I'd really rather have pizza.

WHITEFACE: Bread. Stick to the script. *(To AUGUSTE)* So do it — Yah-da-da-da-dah ...

AUGUSTE: *(Shrugs. He thinks the whole thing is nuts. Speaks to TRAMP.)* **Hungry, man? Take these stones and make bread, yah-da-da-da-dah.** *(TRAMP starts to take stones.)*

WHITEFACE: *(Slaps stones away.)* **No! You don't take the stones! You're Jesus — you're above temptation.**

TRAMP: *(Timidly to WHITEFACE)* **Excuse me, but you have us mixed up.** *(Pointing up at AUGUSTE)* **He's above *me!***

WHITEFACE: Oh, keep quiet! *(To AUGUSTE)* **And you — don't say yah-da-da-da-dah.**

AUGUSTE: You did.

WHITEFACE: I'm a director. That's the way to direct. Now, Jesus will not be tempted by stones. *(TRAMP, "acting," shakes head no. WHITEFACE smacks him.)* **So tell the devil out loud!**

TRAMP: You told me to keep quiet. *(WHITEFACE smacks him again. TRAMP looks up at AUGUSTE and speaks.)* **Sorry, friend. Stones will not a pizza make.**

140

WHITEFACE: Bread! It's bread, bread, bread! *(Jerks TRAMP to his feet.)* **Get up. We have to rehearse the next temptation.** *(Takes him to stepstool.)* **Climb up there.** *(TRAMP climbs.)* **This is the temple in Jerusalem.** *(To AUGUSTE)* **You tell him to jump off.**

AUGUSTE: **That's stupid. He'd jump right into traffic.**

WHITEFACE: **Don't ever say that again! Nothing in the Bible is stupid. You hear me? Nothing!**

AUGUSTE: *(To audience)* **I wouldn't be here if I didn't need the job.** *(To TRAMP)* **OK, Jesus, jump!** *(Smacks TRAMP on the back and he falls off stool.)*

WHITEFACE: **No, no, no! He doesn't jump.**

AUGUSTE: **He doesn't do *anything* I tell him to?**

WHITEFACE: **That's right.**

AUGUSTE: **Then why do I keep trying?**

WHITEFACE: **Because you're the devil.**

AUGUSTE: **The devil I am!**

WHITEFACE: **And you don't know when to quit.**

AUGUSTE: **You got that right.**

WHITEFACE: **OK, so he doesn't jump, yah-da-da-da-dah...** *(Takes TRAMP to stepladder and speaks to AUGUSTE.)* **Now you take him to the top of a tall mountain.**

TRAMP: *(Still shaken from fall)* **To j-jump?**

WHITEFACE: **You always say, "No." Remember?** *(TRAMP nods apprehensively and climbs ladder, sits on top. WHITEFACE speaks to AUGUSTE.)* **Now you tell him he can have everything he sees if he'll worship you.**

AUGUSTE: *(Peers out at audience.)* **I don't see anything out there anyone would want.**

WHITEFACE: **Act, stupid. *Act!***

AUGUSTE: **You said nothing in the Bible is stupid.**

WHITEFACE: **The Bible's not stupid — *you* are! Now, get on with it. There's not much time left.**

AUGUSTE: *(Picks up speed.)* **OK.** *(Points to audience.)* **See all that, Jesus? Yah-da-da-da-dah.**

TRAMP: *(Catches on to "acting" and shakes head.)* **Don't want any! No, no, no!**

(AUGUSTE begins dancing around stage singing "Yah-da-da-da-dah" and TRAMP sings "No, no, no." This makes WHITEFACE furious.)

WHITEFACE: *(Yells over the din.)* **What do you think you're doing? This is a play, not a goofy *opera*!** *(Goes to AUGUSTE and stomps on his toe.)* **And you're no singer!**

TRAMP: *(Comes back to reality and jumps off ladder.)* **He's no devil either. *You're* the devil.** *(Pops one of WHITEFACE's balloons with his pin.)*

WHITEFACE: *(Leaps into air and screams.)* **Yeow! You're fired! You're both fired!**

AUGUSTE: Wrong. We do know when to *quit*. *(To TRAMP)* **Let's go, Buddy.**

WHITEFACE: You won't get paid!

TRAMP: *(Gathers up a few stones from floor.)* **Not to worry. I'm Jesus, remember?** *(Holds up stones.)* **We're going to the park and have pizza!** *(TRAMP and AUGUSTE exit.)*

WHITEFACE: *(Turns to audience and sighs.)* **Ohhh ... why is it so hard to teach a simple Bible lesson?** *(Exits.)*

142

The Summons

by David W. Lloyd (*Cop a Plea and Poppatui*) **and the Faith and Fantasy Group of the Seekers Faith Community of the Church of the Saviour**

CONFIDENTIAL! DO NOT TELL ANYONE IN ADVANCE!

CAST: A troupe of CLOWNS.

PROPS: Sticks, copies of summonses with gold seals, crown of thorns. NO MUSIC OR SIGNS.

COSTUME: Black/navy turtleneck sweaters, black/navy slacks, whiteface make-up with no colors.

Clowns assemble in secret to change into costume and make-up, to be ready at the end of the sermon. Just as benediction is about to be given, clowns burst unannounced into sanctuary with sticks and threatening gestures and give each person in the congregation a summons. Several clowns seize the pastor, co-pastor, and other worship leaders. One clown places crown of thorns lightly on the pastor's head. Pastors and leaders are pulled and pushed, so that they are always off-balance, out of sanctuary. All clowns quickly exit, leaving the congregation leaderless.

Clowns leave church building together immediately to change out of costume. *Do not mingle with the congregation after the service.*

Then, on *Easter morning,* **place pardons** (*Scripted and gold-sealed*) **on every seat in the sanctuary before the altar preparation committee, choir, and congregation arrive.**

Summons
Sanhedrin of Palestine

In The Matter Of

<u>Jesus of Nazareth</u> et alia

You are hereby commanded to appear before the Sanhedrin, sitting at the home of Caiaphas the High Priest, on or before _____ to answer to the following charge(s):

1. Aiding and abetting Jesus of Nazareth and others in blasphemy;
2. Profaning the Sabbath by reaping and threshing grain;
3. Aiding and abetting Jesus of Nazareth in profaning the Sabbath, to wit: assisting in the practice of medicine on that day;
4. Aiding and abetting Jesus of Nazareth in committing impurities, to wit: using Samaritan utensils, association with lepers, touching corpses, and other similar acts without thereafter being purified by a priest;
5. Conspiracy of sedition.

Witness, the hand of Caiaphas, High Priest of the Sanhedrin of Palestine, this _____ day of _____.

_____
Caiaphas

Pardon

卍卍卍卍卍卍卍卍卍卍卍卍卍卍卍卍卍卍

In consideration of the recent arrest and crucifixion of the Galilean, Jesus, for religious blasphemy and insurrection against Rome, it is unnecessary for further investigation into your actions. You are therefore pardoned.

this___ day of _____

_____
Caiaphas

A Clown Processional
by Janet Litherland

Let a troupe of clowns dress in their clown finery and parade into the sanctuary during the prelude on Palm Sunday morning. Each clown should have a big, homemade palm branch to wave. *(Use green construction paper for the fronds and pipe cleaner or stiff cardboard for the stem. Tape or wire a florist's pick to end of stem.)* Clowns also carry balloon figures, stickers, paper hearts — something to give away.

As they enter, they take turns shouting, "Hosanna!" They also stop to invite children of the congregation to join them in the march. *(Take time with this entry, helping children to exit pews and enter aisles.)* Depending on size of troupe, have one or two large urns in chancel area, wherever the flower arrangements are to be placed, with a big chunk of Styrofoam in each pot. As clowns and children arrive up front, clowns *(With help of children)* stick their palm branches into the Styrofoam, creating, on the spot, the Palm Sunday "arrangement(s)."

Each child is then given one of the above-mentioned clown gifts and escorted back to pew. As prelude concludes, each clown joins his or her own family, sitting within the congregation.

Minister reads: "The great crowd that had come for the Feast heard that Jesus was on his way to Jerusalem. They took palm trees and went out to meet him, shouting, 'Hosanna! Blessed is he who comes in the name of the Lord! Blessed is the King of Israel!' " (John 12:12-13, NIV)

Service begins.

Jedidiah Becomes a Clown

Based on I Corinthians 4:8-14; Acts 2:1-21

by Tim Morrison
(Kujo)

AUTHOR'S NOTE: This is a sermon, which the Reverend
Tim Morrison preaches, seated before the congregation,
applying his clown make-up — transforming himself from
ordinary mortal to clown minister: The new birth, the
"Easter" of his life! It is a much-requested performance.

Long, long ago, Scripture relates that God, in God's
gentle fashion, took a clod, a lump of earth, breathed
his spirit into it, and made something wonderful happen. Well, friends, the words "clown" and "clod" come
from the same root word. Clod, a clump of earth; clown,
a rather lumpish fellow.

Jedidiah had not always been a clown. In fact, as
a lad growing up in Jerusalem, he had never even entertained thoughts of being a clown. He had heard of court
jesters and fools, but he knew that very few people ever
became such. Jedidiah planned to become a merchant
as his father was; instead, he became a clown, the *first*
clown, perhaps — all because of him, because of Jesus
of Nazareth.

Jedidiah was very, very sad. Life seemed dark and
foreboding. All joy was gone. Jedidiah was a follower of
Jesus; in fact, Jedidiah believed, along with many
others, that Jesus was the Messiah, the one who brought
fulfillment to the kingdom of God. Now Jesus lay dead
in the tomb. He had been crucified on a cross like a
common criminal. The sadness that Jedidiah felt was
overwhelming. He decided that he must mourn the
death of Jesus, the one who had brought so much hope
into his life and into the lives of others. To show the
depth of his grief and sadness, Jedidiah marked his face

with ashes. He sought to make his flesh appear white, so that there would be no mistaking that he wore the mask of death, of grief, of sadness.

As he whitened his face, Jedidiah remembered the days, not so very long ago, when he had first become a follower of Jesus. Many friends had come to Jedidiah to tell him of a new teacher named Jesus who traveled the area. This Jesus brought hope to all who heard him. There was an aura of joy about him. At first Jedidiah merely scoffed. There had been reports of other teachers like this before. But with this Jesus, the intrigue and talk persisted. People spoke of consistency in all that Jesus shared — of peace, of forgiveness, of love, and of eternal life.

One Sabbath Jedidiah heard that Jesus was at a nearby synagogue, so he went to see the man for himself. Jedidiah was awed by Jesus' presence. There was something unique about this man. He observed in amazement as Jesus cured the hand of a paralyzed man, while the Pharisees looked on in disgust. Later, Jedidiah watched as the people clamored for another miracle. He heard Jesus refuse, saying, "The only miracle you will be given is the miracle of the prophet Jonah." Jesus said something about three days and three nights in the depths of the earth, but Jedidiah wasn't sure what that meant; nonetheless, he continued in awe of the teacher.

Jedidiah thrilled in the teachings of the master, especially in the parables, as Jesus shared through them the glory of the kingdom of God, the hope for the poor and downtrodden, the oppressed. Jesus talked of love and forgiveness. Jedidiah heard the teacher's plea that the people repent, believe and trust in the Lord God. To Jedidiah, these words, these teachings, brought so much more hope and meaning to life than did the way of the Pharisees — observing an endless list of laws and rules.

With time, Jedidiah and many others began to be-lieve that Jesus was the Christ, the son of the living God, sent to redeem Israel. Joy filled the lives of the followers of Jesus. Just seven short days before, Jedidiah had joined with many others to welcome Jesus into Jerusalem, the Holy City. Why, the people had shouted for joy, waved palm fronds, and then laid them and their cloaks down upon the road for Jesus to ride over during his triumphant entry. They welcomed their king who would bring them life and fulfillment through God. Now Jesus was dead; he had been crucified and entombed. So Jedidiah put on his ashen face, the mask of death, so that he might proclaim his sorrow to all the world. And he went to the tomb to mourn, to be close to the one who had given him so much hope, so much joy.

What was that which Jedidiah saw in the distance? Two women coming toward him ... and ... and they were happy! No, they were ecstatic! It was Mary Mag-dalene and the other Mary! How could this be? How could they be so joyous? As they came near him on the road, they cried out, "Rejoice, brother! Take off that mask of death and put on a new face. We have seen the Lord. He is risen! We're going to tell the disciples!" And the women continued on their way.

Jedidiah was dumbfounded. What had they said? ... Take off the mask of death, put on the new face, for we have seen the Lord ... He is risen?! Jedidiah rushed to where the body had been laid, and, indeed, the grave was empty! Then Jedidiah remembered the words that Jesus had spoken on several occasions. He had told them that he must go to Jerusalem where he would be arrested, would suffer and die, but that he would rise again in glory. It was true. It was true! Jesus had kept his word. His teaching was true, for he was alive again!

Suddenly, Jedidiah felt surging within himself a new life, a new vitality, and hope. He thought once more of the words of the women ... put on a new face. He would. He would, indeed, put on a new face, but he would put it on over his white face, his mask of death. "For," Jedidiah thought, "I can become a visual reminder of coming from death to life. I will have a big smile, with wide-open eyes and rosy cheeks. I want to be full of life, to be full of hope and joy. Yes, I want to show that Jesus has conquered death. The tomb was empty where he had been laid. Jesus has brought life and the fulfillment of God's kingdom!"

And so Jedidiah became a special kind of jester. He became a clown, the first clown, perhaps, to use whiteface. When Jedidiah spoke and taught, he wore the whiteface, the mask of death, but always over it was that happy, smiling face, that face so full of life and hope. Jedidiah took to heart Jesus' message to do as even Jesus had done — to be a servant of God through Christ by bringing joy and happiness to all whom he met — to be a servant, each to the other.

Now Jedidiah had a message to share. He found that by being a fool, a fool for Christ's sake, people listened to him, if only for the novelty of it. But many who listened also became believers in Jesus as the Christ. Oh, what joy that was for Jedidiah! What peace he knew as he shared the wonderful message that had brought him his face: Christ had risen, he had conquered the grave, Christ had risen, indeed!

And that, my friends, is how Jedidiah became a clown, a fool for Christ's sake.

The Resurrection
Based on John 20:1-18

by Stephen Ashcroft
(Ludo the Clown)

CAST: Five clowns — SERGEANT MAJOR, OFFICER, three TROOPERS: Characters — GHOST, MARY MAGDALENE, CHRIST.

SETTING: Bare acting area or structure at back center to represent tomb. Or, altar may represent tomb.

SERGEANT MAJOR: *(Off-stage)* **Quick march! Sinister ... dexter ... sinister ... dexter ... sinister.**

(Enter SERGEANT MAJOR and TROOPERS. Comic drill — last TROOPER in line is completely inept.)

OFFICER: *(Enters.)* **Sergeant Major! What do you call this rabble?**

SERGEANT MAJOR: **I don't call them, sir, but they come anyway. Detail reporting for guard duty, sir!**

OFFICER: **Very well. Your orders are to guard this area. Be particularly vigilant!**

TROOPER 1: **But this is a graveyard, sir.**

TROOPER 2: **Who'd want to get in here at night?**

TROOPER 3: **I don't want to come in here at any time.**

OFFICER: **That's enough! You have your orders. Pay special attention to that tomb. There's an important personage inside. Report to me in the morning.** *(Exit)*

SERGEANT MAJOR: **OK, lads, spread out there.**
(TROOPERS huddle closer together.)

TROOPER 1: **I don't like this, do you?**

TROOPER 2: **No. It's spooky.**

TROOPER 1: **I'm scared of spooks — ghosties and ghoulies,**

TROOPER 2:   And long-legged beasties . . .

TROOPER 3:   And things that go bump . . .

SERGEANT MAJOR: Well, you go bump into everything, soldier, and no one's scared of you. Still, I know what you mean, lads. What we need is a singsong to keep our spirits up. Come on.

(SERGEANT MAJOR and TROOPERS line up across stage and begin singing. GHOST enters, creeps up behind TROOPER 3, taps him on shoulder. TROOPER 3 runs off, GHOST exits, and singing peters out.)

SERGEANT MAJOR: Now where's he gone? Never mind. I'll deal with him in the morning. Come now, after me.

(Process is repeated until only SERGEANT MAJOR is left. He asks audience what happened. Doesn't believe them about GHOST. "No, it wasn't; yes, it was," etc. Asks audience to tell him if GHOST returns. GHOST enters, and audience tells. Business as CLOWN wants. [He doesn't believe the audience; GHOST moves when he turns, so he cannot see it; maybe GHOST and SERGEANT MAJOR do a "peek-a-boo" routine, never seeing each other, etc.] Eventually, SERGEANT MAJOR and GHOST come face to face. Both scream and run off in different directions. Lights dim to achieve change of mood.)

MARY MAGDALENE: *(Enters and approaches tomb. Finds it empty and turns away in tears. CHRIST enters and MARY speaks without looking at him.)* **Who's there? Are you the gardener? Please leave me alone, whoever you are.**

CHRIST: Mary.

MARY: You!

CHRIST: Don't touch me. Aren't you afraid of me, Mary?

MARY: Of you? How could I be?

CHRIST: But you saw me die.

MARY: Why should I fear death now?

CHRIST: I have conquered death. Can you believe that?

MARY: Of course.

CHRIST: Then go and tell the others.

MARY: Yes ... yes, I will.

(MARY and CHRIST exit in different directions. Lights up for mood change. SERGEANT MAJOR and OFFICER enter from different directions. SERGEANT MAJOR tries to creep off unnoticed, but fails.)

OFFICER: Sergeant Major! Come here and explain yourself.

SERGEANT MAJOR: It's not my fault, sir. I tried to keep her out.

OFFICER: Out, Sergeant Major? You weren't there to keep someone out. You were there to keep someone *in!*

SERGEANT MAJOR: In, sir?

OFFICER: In, Sergeant Major. You remember the very important personage in the tomb? He got out. Explain that, Sergeant Major! ... I'm waiting.

SERGEANT MAJOR: Act of God, sir?

OFFICER: Don't waste my time.

SERGEANT MAJOR: Trained worms, sir. They crawled into the tomb, lifted the body on their backs and crawled out with it ... sir?

OFFICER: Sergeant Major!

SERGEANT MAJOR: *(Desperately)* Conjuring tricks with bones?

OFFICER: Hmmm ... Conjuring tricks with bones. I like that, Sergeant Major. I like that. You might even find the odd bishop who'd believe that one.

SERGEANT MAJOR: He'd have to be a very odd

bishop, sir.
OFFICER: Never mind. Come on, we'll tell Pilate. *(Exit)*

Seeing Is Believing

by Tommy Thomson
(Clownbo)

CAST: One CLOWN, one MIME.

MIME SKETCH: Mime moves across stage, creating an invisible wall with hands and movement.

Clown enters, out for a walk, and sees Mime working. Gives audience a glance that says, "Will you look at this!" and watches for a few seconds, until Mime moves away from Clown's chosen spot.

Clown moves cautiously toward invisible wall. He stretches out hand with finger pointing, to touch wall. It passes through, as does hand, arm, and all of him. Now Clown is standing on same side of wall as Mime.

Clown watches for a few more brief seconds, then edges over to Mime and taps his or her shoulder.

Mime turns to Clown, and Clown gestures that there is no wall there, as he has just walked through it. Mime shakes head, "Yes, wall is there," and does a few movements with hands to show Clown. Then Mime motions to Clown to copy what he is doing with hands. Clown is a bit stiff at first, but eventually his movement becomes smoother, like that of Mime. Both move along for short bit, creating wall.

Clown stops, turns to Mime, both smile and shake hands, then wave, "Bye, bye." As Clown turns to walk through the imaginary wall, he hits it full frontal and falls back, knocked out by the clash. Mime looks at fallen Clown, shrugs shoulders, smiles, then continues creating imaginary wall

until Off-stage *(Or freezes at side, after going as far as possible).*

ROUND OFF: There are many out there who don't know God and can't see him in the world. But he is there, sustaining his creation. Part of our task is to reveal the Living God through our actions and words to such people . . . Amen.

APRIL FOOL'S DAY
(See also "The Banana Illusion," page 236)

April Foolishness

by Janet Litherland

CAST: Four CLOWNS.

PROPS: Two balloons, pin, large doughnut (real), two clown tricks.

OPENING: CLOWN 1 enters carrying balloon. He is followed closely by CLOWN 2 (also carrying balloon) who shadows CLOWN 1's steps and actions exactly, like "second skin." (Play this out for laughs.) CLOWN 1 is oblivious until CLOWN 2 makes a mistake, bumping into CLOWN 1, scaring him into a "Yeow!" CLOWN 1 turns and finds himself face-to-face with CLOWN 2.

CLOWN 2: **April Fool!** *(Turns and starts walking other way. CLOWN 1 moves in close behind, reversing the shadowing, but CLOWN 2 is wise to it.)* **I know you're there.** *(Does a couple of fancy steps that CLOWN 1 shadows.)*

CLOWN 1: *(Peering at CLOWN 2's ears)* **Say, did you know you have a terrible case of earlobes?** *(CLOWN 2 grabs his own ears.)* **April Fool!** *(CLOWN 2 tries to land a back-handed punch on CLOWN 1's stomach, but CLOWN 1 ducks and the punch misses.)* **Sorry, but I was expecting that.**

CLOWN 2: **But you aren't expecting *this!*** *(Pops CLOWN 1's balloon with pin. CLOWN 1 yells in fright and runs off.)* **April Fool!**

(CLOWN 3 enters with big doughnut.)

CLOWN 2: **Hey! That looks good! Where'd you get it?**
CLOWN 3: **Down at the church. The Youth fellowship is giving them away free.**
CLOWN 2: **Free? Great!** *(Runs off.)*
CLOWN 3: *(To audience)* **That's true, but I got the last**

one! April Fool! *(Takes a big bite.)*

CLOWN 4: *(Enters.)* **Hi! Gee, I hope you didn't get that doughnut from the Youth Fellowship.** *(CLOWN 3 nods, his mouth stuffed full.)* **Well, I heard they made them with soap powder instead of flour.** *(CLOWN 3 grabs his stomach and runs off.)* **April Fool!**

CLOWN 4: *(To audience)* **OK, so we're pretty foolish. But the Bible tells us in I Corinthians 4:10 that we are fools for Christ's sake. We love him and follow him so that others will come to love and follow him, too. Sometimes we're serious fools; sometimes just plain silly fools, like on April Fool's Day; but we are always fools for Christ.**

Would you like to know how April Fool's Day got started? *(Gets them to encourage him/her as he tells and "acts out" his story.)* **OK, it was like this: April Fool's Day was invented by clowns** *(Models "self")*, **who always love a good joke.** *(Does trick.)* **Several years ago, a whole bunch of clowns were building a big barn where they could practice their foolishness.** *(Does another trick.)* **As it happened, they were all left-handed.** *(Shows.)* **Well, they dug the land** *(Shows)* **and poured the foundation** *(Shows)* **just fine, but when they started to put the walls together, their work came to a screeching** *(Screeches)* **halt. You know why? . . . Because they didn't have even one left-handed hammer!**

Well, the unfinished barn became known as the April Folly, because it had been abandoned by fools on the first day of April — thus, April Fool's Day. *(Takes bow and starts to exit.)* **. . . And if you believe even one word of that, you're the biggest fools of all!** *(Exits.)*

Rules to Remember

by Janet Litherland

CAST: Two CLOWNS.

PROPS: Bicycle, helmet, snap-on wheel reflectors in pocket of Clown 1, clown "rule" book clearly marked "Bicycle Safety."

OPENING: Bicycle is parked center, helmet on floor beside it. CLOWN 1 is standing beside bike, memorizing rules, when CLOWN 2 enters.

CLOWN 2:   *(Really impressed with bike, he circles it and whistles.)* **Man, that's a nice bike!**

CLOWN 1:   **Thanks.** *(Continues studying.)*

CLOWN 2:   *(Rubs the handlebars.)* **Sure would like to have a bike like that!**

CLOWN 1:   **I just got it. It was a present.**

CLOWN 2:   **Really? Well, why aren't you riding it?**

CLOWN 1:   **Got to learn bicycle safety rules first.** *(CLOWN 2 snickers.)* **What's so funny?**

CLOWN 2:   **Man, if that was my bike, I'd be out there melting down the road like hot fudge on ice cream!**

CLOWN 1:   **That wouldn't be very smart. You could hurt yourself or someone else.** *(Hands CLOWN 2 the rule book.)* **Here, quiz me. They're all true or false.** *(Encourages children in audience to help if he gets stuck. NOTE: Be open to dialog with children.)*

CLOWN 2:   *(Shrugs, then begins quiz.)* **When you're learning to drive, practice in traffic so you can get used to it.** *(CLOWN 1 and children answer — "False!")* **Use your left hand to signal for turns and stops.** *(Answer — "True!")* **Bike drivers don't have to follow signs.** *(Answer — "False!")* **Walk your bike at busy corners.** *(Answer — "True!")* **Look in all directions before**

159

entering the street. *(Answer — "True!")* **Drive in the same direction as the cars are going.** *(Answer — "True!" CLOWN 2 returns book to CLOWN 1.)* **Pretty good. I guess you know the rules.**

CLOWN 1: **Just a couple more things . . .** *(Takes reflectors from pocket and snaps them onto wheels.)* **These are so I can be seen at night.** *(Picks up helmet.)* **And this is to keep me from getting a head injury if I have a wreck.** *(He turns to audience and primps for the children as he puts on his terrific new helmet, unaware that CLOWN 2 is stealing his bike. Children will try to tell him, but he doesn't understand. CLOWN 2 mimes for children to be quiet and not tell as he sneaks — big "tiptoes" — off. Finally, CLOWN 1 realizes what is happening and yells at CLOWN 2 just before he gets away.)* **Hey, you! Come back here with my bike!**

CLOWN 2: **You forgot the most important rule!**

CLOWN 1: **What's that?**

CLOWN 2: **Keep your bike locked with a chain and padlock when you're not watching it!** *(Exits quickly with bike.)*

CLOWN 1: **Hey!** *(Stomps his feet and carries on like a troll. Suddenly stops, remembering something nice, and speaks to audience.)* **But he won't get away with it! I remembered to register my bike with the police department. They etched a number on it that will identify it as *mine!*** *(Starts off.)* **I'm going to get it back!** *(Exits.)*

Three Walkarounds

by Janet Litherland

LITTER

Two clowns: One is a litterbug, dropping endless "stuff" as he/she goes — notes, wrappers, banana peel *(While eating banana)*, **comb** *(After combing hair)*, **wristwatch** *(After looking at time)* — use imagination. Second clown follows, picking up after first clown. He/she pulls a wagon with a trash bag on it. The wagon bears a sign that says, "Litter Buggy."

RECYCLING

One clown with a unicycle: Does his/her "act" along a line about 16 to 20 feet long. When finished, gets off unicycle, walks it back to starting place, gets on and goes over the same line again. The "act" may change slightly, but never the line. A sign on clown's back says: "I'm 'Re-Cycling.' It's good for the environment!"

CONSERVATION

Two clowns: Johnny *(Or Joannie)* **Appleseed** wears a name-identifying sign subtitled, "Save the Earth — Plant trees!" Partner is Billy *(Or Bonnie)* **Birdseed** with name-identifying sign subtitled, "Save the birds — They're worth it!" Both clowns perform their own specialty tricks, taking the opportunity to pass out seeds and talk about conservation.

STEWARDSHIP SUNDAY
(see also Arbor/Bird/Earth Day)

Parable of the Clown Talents

Based on Matthew 25

by Janet Tucker
(Jelly Bean)

CAST: Four CLOWNS and NARRATOR.

PROPS: Suitcase with sign on the outside saying "Hollywood or Bust" with eight gift boxes inside. Five boxes for CLOWN 2 contain: 1. a hand puppet, 2. balloons for sculpturing, 3. a small magic trick, 4. a kazoo, and 5. three balls for juggling. Two boxes for CLOWN 3 contain: 1. three balloons for juggling, 2. one love balloon. One box for CLOWN 4 contains: one love balloon. Also needed: Hawaiian shirt, big clown sunglasses.

OPENING: NARRATOR has large clown prop book titled, "Parable of the Clown Talents" and reads from it throughout the program, pausing as the clowns' actions follow the story.

NARRATOR: Today our parable is from the gospel of Matthew, Chapter 25. Jesus told a lot of great stories, and because they teach us a lesson, we call them parables. In this story, he talks about "talents." When Jesus walked on this earth, a talent was a thing of great worth and value, a piece of money that some people say would be worth $1,500 today. We also use the word "talents" to mean things of great worth and value, such as a talent to sing, play the piano, be a ballerina, play baseball or football. Each of us has a talent of some sort, and all of us have a talent to show love to one another. Let's look now at Matthew 25:14 and see what talents clowns have.

**   "For it will be as when a 'clown' going on a long journey** *(CLOWN 1 enters with suitcase)* **called his**

162

clown friends *(CLOWN 1 calls CLOWNS 2, 3, 4, who come in)* **and entrusted to them his 'clown props.' "** *(CLOWNS now talk about CLOWN 1; going to Hollywood to be a big star — his suitcase says "Hollywood or bust." He opens the case and begins to distribute gift boxes — five to CLOWN 2, two to CLOWN 3, and one to CLOWN 4, as NARRATOR continues.)*

"To one clown friend he gave five clown talents — puppets, animal balloon sculptures, magic, music, and love." *(Gift boxes contain hand puppet, balloons for sculpturing, any small magic trick, kazoo, and love balloon.)*

"To another clown friend he gave two clown talents — juggling and love." *(Three balls and a love balloon)*

"To another clown friend he gave one clown talent — love." *(CLOWN 4 receives just one gift and looks envious, then angry, then puzzled, as NARRATOR continues.)*

"To each was given according to his ability . . . then he went away." *(CLOWN 1 now leaves room, waving and promising to send postcards from Hollywood.)*

"He who had received the five talents began to clown around and use them to spread joy and laughter." *(CLOWN 2 opens each gift box, takes out the item and uses it. He makes the puppet sing "Jesus Loves Me," makes a balloon animal, does the magic trick, plays a song on the kazoo, and blows up the love balloon. CLOWNS 2 and 3 play with the love balloon.)*

"He who had received the two talents also began to use them, as clown talents are intended to bring laughter and love to others." *(CLOWN 3 does the "How to Juggle" routine, finally juggling the balls, and blows up the love balloon. CLOWNS 2 and 3 play with the love balloon.)*

163

"The one who had received the one talent, however, felt he should protect what had been entrusted to him, *(CLOWN 4 thinks hard, then sits on box)* so he sat on it." Surely you've heard of people who sit on their talents!

"Now after a long time, the Master Clown returned from his trip *(CLOWN 1 comes back in a wild tropical print shirt and big clown sunglasses)* and checked on how his clown talents were being used to make the world a happier place. *(CLOWN 2 demonstrates each gift for CLOWN 1, showing him how he's used the talents.)* To the clown using the five talents, he said, 'Well done, good and faithful friend.' "

(CLOWN 3 demonstrates each gift for CLOWN 1.) "To the clown using the two talents, he said, 'Well done, good and faithful friend.' "

(CLOWN 1 now goes to CLOWN 4, who is sitting on the floor.) "To the clown who had received the one talent and was sitting on it, he said, 'Beep, beep.' " That's censored, folks!

Now our story could end here, but clown talents are meant to be used and shared, as are all the talents the Lord has blessed each of YOU with. Let's see if we can encourage our clown friend to use his talent of love. *(NARRATOR and CLOWNS 1, 2, and 3 all recite Bible verses relating to "love" until CLOWN 4 is finally convinced. CLOWN 4 opens his gift and does the "How to Blow Up a Balloon" routine. When he finally gets it blown up, everyone plays with it.)*

Now, as our parable closes, remember Jesus' words in verse 29: "For to everyone who has will be given more and he will have an abundance. Whoever does not have, even what he has will be taken from him." (NIV) Use the "talent for love" God has blessed each of you with, and you will have abundance!

(CLOWNS now take the three love balloons and share them with the audience, giving hugs, or just batting the balloons around.)

MOTHER'S DAY
(and Other Days)

Three Short Skits

by Kay Turner
(Sweet Pea)

LITTLE BIRD TOLD

CAST: Two CLOWNS.

CLOWN 1: *(To CLOWN 2)* **My mom always seems to know when I've done something wrong.**

CLOWN 2: **Then be bad when she's not looking.**

CLOWN 1: **No ... She says a little bird tells her.**

CLOWN 2: **What have you done to make the birds mad at you?**

CLOWN 1: **I don't know, but that's not all. She also told me that God made it so that moms and dads know everything about their kids.**

CLOWN 2: **No ... Not *everything*, huh?**

CLOWN 1: **Yeah! It was bad enough knowing the birds were against me, but now God is watching me, too!**

FED BY THE WORD

CAST: One CLOWN (as service "interrupter"), MINISTER.

PROPS: Large spoon, fork, bib.

SETTING: MINISTER is speaking from pulpit. CLOWN enters, wearing bib and carrying spoon and fork, looking around.

MINISTER: **Excuse me, Clown! Can I help you?**

CLOWN: **Yes. I was told that if I came in here, I would be fed by the Word.**

MINISTER: That is correct.

CLOWN: I wasn't sure how prepared I was expected to be, so I just brought my own utensils. Now, where is the food?

MINISTER: That's not the kind of feeding we were talking about.

CLOWN: Well, nobody needs to feed me. I can do it all by myself.

MINISTER: Wait, Clown. We said you would be fed by the Word, meaning God would speak to you.

CLOWN: OK. I'll just sit here and wait. As soon as you give the word, I'm ready to eat!

CLOSER TO GOD

CAST: One CLOWN (as "interrupter"), MINISTER.

PROP: Sturdy chair.

(CLOWN enters carrying chair and ignores the actions going on around him. He looks upward as he moves about the room, carefully checking for the desired location to place the chair. He finally places it, then looks upward again and shakes his head. He moves chair to another location. He repeats the placement check by looking upward and then down, as if following a path down to the chair. He shakes head and moves chair once again, this time placing it in front of audience. Once chair is set and location check has been verified, he carefully steps up on chair and displays great satisfaction. Keeps checking upward to be sure position is still correct.)

MINISTER: *(To CLOWN)* What are you doing?

CLOWN: I'm trying to get closer to God.

167

A Tribute to Mothers

by *Janet Litherland*

CAST: NARRATOR (either young teenager or puppet), four CLOWNS.

PROPS: Baby carriage, big baby bonnet, bib, two baby bottles, ABC book, juggling balls, big key ring, tricycle, table, rocking chair, money (few bills), stack of books, big eyeglasses, briefcase.

SETTING: NARRATOR reads from lectern at side of stage; table and chair are Upstage Center; stack of books and eyeglasses are on table; briefcase is on floor beside table; CLOWNS are silent, shadowing the narration, except as specified in script.

NARRATOR: Tonight *(Or today)* **we would like to present a tribute to mothers, in observance of Mother's Day, a holiday that started in 1907 when a girl named Anna Jarvis asked her church to hold a special service for all mothers in memory of her mother. Mothers, you know, are those wonderful, warm, hard-to-figure-out creatures essential to everyone's life.**

Membership in the Maternal Order of Motherhood, of course, requires a woman and her offspring. *(FEMALE CLOWN enters, pushing baby carriage, which holds a full-size clown who wears a big baby bonnet and bib.)* **Mothers are always proud of their babies and love to show them off . . . Besides being cute and cuddly, babies need a lot of care** *(BABY cries, "Waaaaaah")*, **and mothers always know what to do.** *(MOTHER shoves bottle in BABY's mouth and wheels carriage across stage, exiting.)*

But before Mom hardly has time to blink, Baby has become a child, needing a different kind of

mother's love — a little more patience, a little more understanding . . . *(MOTHER enters with CHILD, actually the same full-size clown who was BABY. MOTHER has CHILD by the hand and CHILD clutches ABC book. MOTHER sits in chair with CHILD on her lap — crunch!)*

CHILD: *(Reads aloud.)* **A, B, C, D, E, F** . . . *(Can't get last letter. MOTHER points to it, encouraging.)* **E, F,** . . . **E, F, T!** *(MOTHER shakes head no.)* **E, F** . . . **V!** *(MOTHER shakes head no.)* **A, B, C, D, E, F, P!** *(MOTHER shakes head no. CHILD's face brightens.)* **A, B, C, D, E, F, G!** *(MOTHER hugs CHILD and hands him juggling balls. They exit at side opposite their entrance, CHILD trying to juggle, MOTHER helping.)*

NARRATOR: **And then it seems in one more blink of an eye, the child, who needed a little more patience and a little more understanding, has become a teenager, who needs a *lot* more patience and a *lot* more understanding!** . . . *(MOTHER enters, followed by TEENAGER — same clown as CHILD — who is asking, begging, pleading for something. Finally, MOTHER takes keys out of pocket and hands them reluctantly to TEENAGER, who snatches them and runs. MOTHER drops into chair.)* . . . **Ah, yes, good reason for Mother to worry — the keys to the car.** *(TEENAGER enters on tricycle and "zooms" across stage, waving to MOTHER as he/she exits.)*

Then one day the teenager becomes a young adult, ready to go out into the world, either to college, or to work . . . *(YOUNG ADULT enters, gives MOTHER a patronizing hug, waves, and exits on other side. MOTHER sits in chair.)* **The young adult really wants to spread his *(Her)* wings, become responsible, be totally on his *(Her)* own** . . . *(YOUNG ADULT rushes in with an urgent request for MOTHER, who pulls money out of her pocket and hands it over. YOUNG*

ADULT thanks her and rushes out.)

And Mother still worries. But this time she looks for something else to do, too. *(MOTHER picks book off stack and begins to read.)* **She takes an interest in things she hasn't had time to do for years — like reading, or an exercise class, or lunch with her friends, or cleaning out the attic and having a yard sale and spending all the money on herself ...**

Then one day her young adult returns, this time with a spouse *(YOUNG ADULT enters with SPOUSE.)* **... and she knows that the offspring she has so carefully nurtured over the years has truly become an adult. She is happy, she is proud, and she feels she has done her job reasonably well.** *(ADULT and SPOUSE exit, waving and blowing kisses.)*

Will Mother stay home and worry? Not this time! Now she can *really* **do something different. She can go to college, or get a job, or both.** *(MOTHER picks up stack of books and puts on eyeglasses.)* **... She can go out into the world and** *fulfill* **herself!** *(MOTHER picks up briefcase in other hand and exits happily.)* **... And at the end of her long, satisfying day, she can still come home to her comfortable, familiar surroundings ...** *(MOTHER re-enters, puts books and briefcase down, and sits in rocker.)* **... and rock in her favorite chair, remembering all those wonderful years of motherhood.**

But what is that we see on the horizon? *(ADULT and SPOUSE enter with baby carriage that holds another full-size clown wearing bonnet and bib. BABY cries, "Waaaaaah!")* **Of course, Mother is overjoyed and takes great pleasure in her new grandchild ...** *(MOTHER kisses BABY on forehead and BABY cries again.)* **And, of course, since she is so obviously overjoyed, her child and the spouse offer to let her**

baby-sit every single day!

Mother thanks them profusely for their wonderful offer, but this is a "New Wave" Mom who has other ideas ... *(She picks up briefcase and shows it to them.)* She explains that her child and the spouse will raise their own lovely baby, as she did hers ... And she will be happy to baby-sit once in a while ... After work ... After she makes her way through that exhilarating rush-hour traffic ... *(MOTHER starts to exit with briefcase.)* ... She'll give them a call later, if they need advice. She'll even bake cookies and share them right along with her newly discovered tofu salad, if her child and spouse, and baby of course, will come for dinner on Saturday night ...

(MOTHER exits, leaving new family On-stage, staring at one another. Finally, BABY cries loudly and his own MOTHER puts a bottle in his mouth. FATHER pats NEW MOTHER on the back with pride and affection. Family exits on opposite side from ORIGINAL MOTHER.)

And that's the way we have motherhood figured out — all mothers having the opportunity to do it all, from beginning to end. Because they're so good at it! Yes, mothers are those wonderful, warm, *loveable* creatures essential to everyone's life ... God bless mothers everywhere!

PENTECOST
The Gift

by Carolyn Costley
(Spatz & Spatz, Jr.)

CAST: A troupe of CLOWNS.

PROP: Large gift-wrapped box (open at top or with removable lid). Box has big bow made of balloons or toilet tissue, or something "clownish."

BACKGROUND: This silent Pentecost script is based on Acts 2. It interprets God's gift as "love" and uses hugs to represent love.

MIME SKETCH: Confused clowns enter from all over the room. Suddenly notice a large gift-wrapped box on altar and come together in a group.

Group takes a vote, then pushes one *(Elected)* **clown to get the box. Clown takes box to pulpit or other visible location.**

Clown opens box and is thrilled. Holds it for other clowns to peer into.

Clown reaches in and pulls out a hug, showing it to the congregation. *(Use imagination. Chances are, the audience will stare blankly!)*

Group demonstrates by passing hug from clown to clown. *(Use different kinds of hugs: Bear hug, side-by-side shoulder hug, hand clasp, etc. First CLOWN picks up the hug again at the other end.)*

All clowns distribute hugs to congregation. *(Do this in the same way an offering plate is passed, indicating to first person in pew to pass it down the row. Encourage people to move as quickly as possible.)*

PENTECOST

Honest Ananias

Based on Acts 9:10-19

by Roly Bain
(Roly)

CAST: One CLOWN.

PROPS: Unicycle or small clown car, telephone, trombone or other musical instrument, music stand.

CLOWN: *(Enters on unicycle/car. The sound of a phone is heard. After much business and tangle, CLOWN produces the phone from his pocket and answers it.)* **Damascus 123, Honest Ananias at your service. Second-hand camels, best quality Jesus souvenirs, Easter chicks going cheap, Pentecostal whoopee cushions for that rushing mighty wind! . . . Hello, who is it? Don't mess about; who is it really? You can't be God — not on the ordinary phone! . . . Well, yes, I suppose that is the point. Right, God, what can I do for you? . . . God? Help!** *(He kneels, as he suddenly realizes who he's talking to.)* **Ananias at your service, Father . . . Sorry, I was only messing about.**

   Have I heard of Saul? Of course I have. Every-one's heard of Saul, the rotten vindictive little man. A horrible Pharisee, as far as I can see! He's vowed to kill us all. It's no fun being stoned to death, you know.

   He's on his way here? Help! *(Slams receiver and shouts to audience.)* **Everybody hide — he'll kill us all!** *(Sees nobody moving.)* **You are Christians, aren't you?** *(He panics and charges around, falls over; phone rings again.)*

   He's going to Straight Street? *(To audience)* **I'm in Queer Street and he's in Straight Street — ironic, innit!**

173

And he's seen me on the television. He can't have. It hasn't been invented yet! Sorry, he's had a vision ... of me ... I hope it was my best side! And I'm going to lay hands on him ... Too right, I'm going to lay hands on him, the rotten little so-and-so. Then what?

I've got to bless him and give him back his sight? Blind for three days? Good! Serves him right ... Sorry. Yes, I know I've got to love my enemies, but it isn't always easy, you know ... Oh, you do know.

Yes, I've got a chosen instrument. *(Business with trombone and music stand, telling God to hang on a minute. Eventually plays something.)* Did you like it?

Paul is your chosen instrument! Why didn't you say so in the first place? To bring your name to the whole world! Who's Paul? ... Paul is Saul? Saul's Saul! But he's going to be Paul? ... OK, you know best.

And you want me to lay hands on him? Couldn't I just send him a get-well card? ... No. Couldn't I just wave from down the street? I don't trust him, you see ... No. Couldn't I just shout through the letter box? He might stone me, you see. Couldn't I just nod to him in the same room? That's pretty close ... I've got to touch him, lay hands on him to fill him with the Holy Spirit ... What? With *these* hands? *My* hands? Cor! You never know what might happen with the Holy Spirit around ...

You'll show him how much he has to suffer — that's better! Remember Jesus. Of course, I remember Jesus ... Oh, I see. Suffer like he did. Father, this is absolute foolishness, but it's what you want, and I guess your foolishness is wiser than the wisdom of men. Alright, I'll do it. I'm on my way

... What's that? He's saying his prayers. Good! That's a start. I'll see you in Straight Street. Bye!

Flag Etiquette

by Janet Litherland

CAST: NARRATOR clown, two silent clowns — MAGGIE, CHARLIE.

PROPS: U. S. flag, stationary pole with pulley, U. S. flag attached to marching pole, pole receptacle, umbrella, tricycle or clown car, a pennant, bag of marshmallows, small table.

SETTING: Stationary pole is in place, center. Pole receptacle is nearby. NARRATOR reads from script at lectern, Down Left. Table is beside lectern.

OPENING: NARRATOR enters carrying folded flag and flag on marching pole. He places folded flag on table and inserts marching pole into receptacle.

NARRATOR: Hello everybody! . . . *(Today/tomorrow)* **is Flag Day, observed in the United States of America on June 14 every year since 1877. One hundred years earlier, our Continental Congress officially adopted our first flag, and even then, our flag was already over 100 years old. Let's see . . . That means our flag is now over 300 years old! George Washington once said that the "red" was from our mother country, England, and the "white" was there to separate us. The thirteen stars in a blue field represented a new constellation. Of course now we have lots more stars. We have, uh . . . fifty stars!**

    At this time, my colleagues and I would like to teach you some rules about flag ettie-ket — that means how to behave with the flag — so that you will be prepared for Flag Day. *(CLOWNS enter. CHARLIE rides tricycle and carries pennant. MAGGIE holds umbrella over both their heads and carries bag of marshmallows. Both CLOWNS respond to narration in*

176

their own bumbling ways — funny!)

(To CLOWNS) **Park the car, Charlie; and Maggie, why do you have that umbrella? . . . Oh, it's raining outside? Well, it's not raining in here. Put it away. And take your places, both of you . . .**

(To audience) **We'll start with carrying the flag in a parade.** *(Gives marching flag to MAGGIE, who tries holding it several ways before getting it right. CHARLIE holds his pennant high.)* **Maggie, you should be on Charlie's right when you march, because our flag is always on the "marching right." It says so right here.** *(CLOWNS march side-by-side.)* **But if there is a whole row of flags, our flag should be in the center and out in front.** *(NARRATOR moves beside CHARLIE. MAGGIE doesn't budge, so NARRATOR pushes her forward between them to demonstrate. They march.)*

(NARRATOR returns to lectern and MAGGIE lays flag on CHARLIE's tricycle.) **No! No! No! Maggie!** *(She reacts.)* **Don't *ever* drape the flag over a vehicle! It says that right here, Section 3b. Pick it up at once!** *(She does, but it touches the ground and NARRATOR yells again. CHARLIE is giggling by this time.)* **No! No! No! Maggie!** *(She reacts.)* **Section 4b — The flag must never touch the ground!** *(MAGGIE snatches it up and shoves it to the laughing CHARLIE to see if he can do better. He holds it correctly.)*

Section 2c — The flag must never be displayed when the weather is in . . . incle . . . inclem . . . *(Gives up.)* **When the weather is *bad*.** *(MAGGIE runs to get her umbrella and tries to hold it over CHARLIE's flag. CHARLIE giggles.)* **No, Maggie, the umbrella won't help. Put it away.** *(She does. Then she stands aside and begins eating her marshmallows.)* **Charlie, put that flag over here, in the pole receptacle.** *(He does.)*

Now we're going to work with a hoisted flag.

You two pick it up and take it to the pole. *(They start to unfold it.)* **Maggie, Maggie, Maggie!** *(MAGGIE jumps, spilling her marshmallows.)* **You mustn't *eat* while handling the flag!** *(She scurries to pick up some of the marshmallows and drops them into the flag CHARLIE is holding between his arms.)* **No! No! No! Maggie!** *(She slips and falls.)* **Section 4h — The flag should never be used as a receptacle for receiving, holding, carrying, or delivering *anything*!** *(CHARLIE flips the marshmallows out of flag and onto MAGGIE, who remains on floor.)*

(To audience) **I must apologize for my colleagues. They're still in training. Charlie, attach that flag to the pole and hoist it.** *(He does, but he hoists it very slowly.)* **Briskly, Charlie! Always hoist the flag briskly!** *(He does.)* **Now show us how to lower it.** *(CHARLIE lowers it briskly.)* **No! No! No! Charlie!** *(Now MAGGIE laughs from her position on the floor.)* **Lower it *slowly*. Always lower the flag slowly. Try again. Up, up, up!** *(He does.)* **Down . . . down . . . down . . .** *(He does.)*

Now let's put it up again and we'll talk about saluting. *(CHARLIE hoists it briskly and MAGGIE laughs again.)* **Maggie! On your feet! Always show respect for the flag.** *(She jumps up and salutes with hand to forehead.)* **No, Maggie. That's the military salute. You aren't in the military, are you?** *(She shakes head.)* **Put your hand over your heart . . . That's right. You, too, Charlie. Now then, *aliens* simply stand at attention. Like this.** *(NARRATOR demonstrates, and CLOWNS poke fun at NARRATOR's being an alien — they are thinking from "outer space.")*

(To audience) **Again, I apologize for my colleagues.** *(MAGGIE and CHARLIE begin to take offense.)* **It's difficult to get good help these days.** *(He begins*

178

rambling.) **Then, when you finally find someone who's willing, they're simply not competent. Either that or they look funny.** *(While he's talking, MAGGIE stuffs a marshmallow in his mouth and CHARLIE hangs the open umbrella over his head. They start to exit with tricycle.)*

(NARRATOR tosses umbrella aside and removes marshmallow, sputtering at CLOWNS.) **You're fired! Better yet, I'm going to fly this flag at *half* mast!** *(He lowers it as they watch.)* **You know what *that* means?** *(They shake heads.)* **It means I'm coming to get you, and when I do, you're gonna be *sorry!*** *(He chases them Off-stage.)*

Honor Thy Father

by Janet Litherland

CAST: Two CLOWNS.

PROPS: Big watch for Clown 2, Two colored marking pens, five signs — "Augustine," "Jerome," "Gregory," "Ambrose," "Thomas Aquinas."

OPENING: CLOWN 1 is hanging signs.

CLOWN 2:   *(Enters.)* **Hey! What are you doing? I thought you were in charge of decorations for Father's Day.**

CLOWN 1:   *(Continues working.)* **Right. That's what I'm doing. Since this is a church, I thought I'd be religious and honor the "Fathers of the Church." Folks will appreciate that, don't you think?**

CLOWN 2:   **I don't think so.**

CLOWN 1:   **No? Then how about the "Fathers of Our Country?" I could change "Gregory" here to "George" without much trouble. And I could paste "Jefferson" over "Aquinas."**

CLOWN 2:   **I don't think so.**

CLOWN 1:   **Well, then . . . what do you "think" about a theme? Like . . . "The Sins of the Fathers."**

CLOWN 2:   **No!**

CLOWN 1:   **Father Christmas? Everyone can identify with him.**

CLOWN 2:   **Not this time.**

CLOWN 1:   **Time! Father Time!**

CLOWN 2:   *(Looks at watch.)* **I think we're running out of time. Listen, we need to honor our *own* fathers. They expect it.**

CLOWN 1:   **Oh! Like "Honor thy father and thy mother"?**

CLOWN 2:   **That's better, only leave Mom out of it. She has her own day. Let's turn these signs over and**

180

make new ones. *(They take signs down, write new words on back, and re-hang them as they proceed.)* **Like this . . .** *(Writes "Patience.")* **Fathers have lots of patience. I know mine does, and I really appreciate it.**

CLOWN 1: **Gotcha!** *(Writes "Kindness.")* **My father is nice to me even when I'm naughty.**

CLOWN 2: *(Aside)* **That's a full-time job!** *(Writes "Teacher.")* **Dad taught me how to drive.**

CLOWN 1: *(Aside)* **Debatable!** *(To CLOWN 2)* **He also taught you right from wrong. Remember that time —**

CLOWN 2: **Shhhh! Don't *tell* that!**

CLOWN 1: *(Writes "Friend.")* **My dad is my best friend.**

CLOWN 2: *(Writes "Refuge.")* **My dad is always there to love and protect me.**

CLOWN 1: **Yeah! "Our refuge in time of need." Hey, that's religious!**

CLOWN 2: **My dad's religious.**

CLOWN 1: **So what happened to you?**

CLOWN 2: ***I'm* religious!**

CLOWN 1: **Just kidding. Oh, I thought of another kind of father we could honor. The Father of —**

CLOWN 2: **No more silly ideas. No Santa Claus, or "Father" of anything! Just *our* fathers.** *(That triggers a thought.)* **Hmmmmm . . . Our fathers? How about this — "Our Father who art in heaven"?**

CLOWN 1: **That's good! You *are* religious!**

CLOWN 2: *(Smacks him.)* **Of course I'm religious.**

CLOWN 1: **Then let's do something really religious to honor all fathers.** *(To audience)* **Everyone out there who is a father, please stand . . . Let's make a joyful noise just for them!** *(Leads in applause.)*

CLOWN 2: **And let's honor "Our Father who art in heaven" in the same way: Make a joyful noise unto the Lord!** *(Leads in more applause.)*

CLOWN 1: **Happy Father's Day!** *(CLOWNS exit.)*

Witness to the Truth

Based on John 5:30-36

by Janet Litherland

This day is celebrated in Europe, South America, and Canada with traditional fires. It stems from John 5:30-36, where Jesus presents John as a "witness to the truth," or someone they know, who testifies on Jesus's behalf. He calls John a "burning and shining light." Hence, the use of fires in celebration. This passage also presents the miracles of Jesus as further evidence that he is who he says he is.

CAST: One SOLO CLOWN, one WALK-ON CLOWN.

PROPS: Solo Clown's own tricks of illusion, a stiff dog harness on a stiff leash ("dogless leash") for Walk-on Clown.

SETTING: SOLO CLOWN talks with audience about Jesus and John the Baptist. His illusions are inserted in the patter. WALK-ON CLOWN enters at end.

SOLO CLOWN: Hi there! Bet you didn't know that tomorrow is a holiday ... Can you guess what holiday it is? ... Hasn't anybody ever heard of St. John the Baptist's Day? ... Well, there really is such a holiday in Europe, South America, and Canada. I guess it just hasn't caught on yet in the United States. But I think it's a good holiday — worth celebrating, though you'll probably have to celebrate after work or after school, because right now I can't see anyone granting an excused absence just because you say, "Oh, I stayed home yesterday because it was St. John the Baptist's Day!"

Jesus liked John the Baptist. In fact, he loved him as a brother, and he said so. Jesus, you know, did lots of miracles when he was here on earth. Now I can't do miracles, but I can do some things that look like miracles. For instance ... *(Does first* *illusion.)* **I can also . . .** *(Does second illusion.)* **Jesus, of course, did** *big* **miracles, like turning water into wine and raising people from the dead. I don't do big things like that — just little things, like this . . .** *(Does third illusion.)*

Well, Jesus said that his miracles proved that he was who he said he was, that is, the Son of God. But he also thought that people would appreciate hearing an ordinary guy, someone they knew and respected, testify on his behalf, too. That someone was John the Baptist. Jesus called him a burning and shining light . . . *(If CLOWN has a light or fire illusion, he does it here.)* **John was a good light for Jesus, and people everywhere enjoyed that light. We, too, are lights for Jesus, at least we** *should* **be, if we really love him.**

Now, about that raising people from the dead business. That would be hard to believe, wouldn't it? Unless you were right there and saw it for yourself. Me, I'm not too keen on ghosts and spooky kinds of things — they make me shake! *(CLOWN shakes all over.)* **But I have the faith to believe they can happen, that Jesus really did raise people from the dead, including himself.**

(Leans toward audience and talks as if sharing a secret.) **There's one thing you need to know about St. John the Baptist's Day: There's an old English superstition that says the ghosts of** *dogs* **walk on St. John's Eve. Now I don't really believe that one! Do you?**

(WALK-ON CLOWN enters from side, guiding his "dogless leash," and crosses stage behind SOLO CLOWN. Audience will start giggling and pointing and telling CLOWN to look behind him. When he finally does, he sees the "ghost," shakes all over, and runs off. WALK-ON

183

CLOWN, oblivious to action, keeps crossing stage until he exits.)

Clowns Will Be Clowns

by Janet Litherland

CAST: Five clowns — DIRECTOR, BELL, JOHN, BILL, NOWAY.

PROPS: None.

OPENING: Clown "DIRECTOR" is assembling four clown "ACTORS" to rehearse an Independence Day play.

DIRECTOR: *(Pulls BELL across stage.)* **You stand here. You are going to be the Liberty Bell.** *(As DIRECTOR moves to next actor, BELL puts arms down and out, simulating bell shape, and begins rocking, side to side. DIRECTOR notices.)* **What are you doing?**

BELL: **I'm a bell. I'm ringing. Ding, dong, ding, dong.**

DIRECTOR: **You're the Liberty Bell, not a ding-a-ling. Hold still!**

BELL: *(Holds still.)* **Isn't the Liberty Bell cracked?**

DIRECTOR: **That's right. You're perfect for the part.** *(Moves to JOHN and places him.)* **Stand here. You're going to be John Hancock.** *(As he moves away, JOHN begins his own version of "sign language" with his hands. DIRECTOR notices.)* **Now what are *you* doing?**

JOHN: **I'm signing the Declaration of Independence. Isn't that what John Hancock did?**

DIRECTOR: **Not that way. Stop that!** *(JOHN stops and DIRECTOR moves to BILL.)* **OK, let's see if you can do your part *right*. You're the Bill of Rights.** *(As he moves away, BILL takes three big side-steps to the right. DIRECTOR notices.)* **What do you think you're doing?**

BILL: *(Takes three more steps to the right, one on each word "right.")* ***Right* to life, *Right* to liberty, *Right* to the pursuit of happiness.**

DIRECTOR: **Don't be a clown!**

BILL: That's what I am. And I have a *right* (Steps) to the pursuit of happiness.

DIRECTOR: If you don't take some steps to the *left* and get back to where I put you, you're going to be *left* out of the play! (*BILL moves back. DIRECTOR approaches NOWAY.*) You stand over there.

NOWAY: No way.

DIRECTOR: What?

NOWAY: I said, no way.

DIRECTOR: You have to do what I say.

NOWAY: No way.

DIRECTOR: Did you read your instructions?

NOWAY: No way.

DIRECTOR: What is this No Way, No Way, No Way stuff?

NOWAY: Isn't this an Independence Day play?

DIRECTOR: You know it is!

NOWAY: (*Proudly*) Well, I'm being independent!

BELL: Good idea! (*Resumes rocking side to side.*)

JOHN: Yeah! (*Resumes "signing."*)

BILL: (*Resumes side-stepping.*) Right! Right! Right!

DIRECTOR: I should have known better than to hire a bunch of clowns. *Anybody* could have done a better job!

BELL, BILL, JOHN, NOWAY: (*Shout*) No Way! (*DIRECTOR throws hands up in air and exits.*)

National Clown Week

(1st week in August)

National Clown Week has been set aside to honor clowns of all kinds and to encourage them to develop and share their wonderfully wacky art. It's a perfect time (and perfect *excuse,* if one is needed) for ministry clowns to offer their services — both in-church and outreach — and to let the world know what it is they *do!*

No specific skits are printed here, because most of the Clown Skits in this book will do nicely, especially those in Chapter 5: "SKITS FOR CLOWNING AROUND, Other Days."

Be wonderful, be wacky, and have fun!

The Beatitudes

Based on Matthew 5:3-10 (NIV)

by Stephen Ashcroft
(Ludo the Clown)

CAST: Three clowns — one AUGUSTE and two others who pretend to be "DECORATORS."

PROPS: Lectern, stepladder, bucket of earth (suitable material that looks like earth but does not turn into mud is available from gardening stores), bucket of water, bucket of slosh (soap suds), protective covering for floor area where clowns will work.

OPENING: AUGUSTE walks to lectern and begins a "straight" reading of the lesson.

AUGUSTE: The lesson is taken from the Gospel according to St. Matthew, Chapter 5, beginning at the third verse. "Blessed are the poor in spirit, for theirs is the kingdom of heaven."

(DECORATORS enter with ladder and buckets and begin to set up immediately behind AUGUSTE.)

AUGUSTE: What's going on?

DECORATOR 1: Don't mind us, mate. The Rev wants the ceiling painted, that's all.

AUGUSTE: On a Sunday morning?

DECORATOR 1: Rates he's offering, we have to fit it in when we can.

AUGUSTE: But we're in the middle of a service. I'm reading the lesson.

DECORATOR 1: Then you get on with it, mate. You won't disturb us. *(Begins climbing ladder, carrying bucket of earth.)*

AUGUSTE: *(Returns to reading.)* **"Blessed are those who mourn, for they will be comforted. Blessed are the meek for they will inherit the earth."**

(DECORATOR 1 drops bucket of earth over AUGUSTE.)

AUGUSTE: **How did that happen?**

DECORATOR 1: *(Descends and brushes off AUGUSTE.)* **Search me, mate. I thought there was paint in that bucket. Never mind, bit of luck, really.**

AUGUSTE: **Luck!**

DECORATOR 1: **You said the poor would inherit the earth. You've got your share a bit early. Well, go on.** *(Indicates congregation.)* **They're waiting.**

AUGUSTE: *(Shaken, but determined)* **"Blessed are those who hunger and thirst for righteousness, for they will be filled."**

DECORATOR 2: **Thirst! Of course! We forgot something.**

(DECORATORS pour water from second bucket down AUGUSTE's trousers.)

AUGUSTE: **Why did you do that?**

DECORATOR 2: **Well, you've got the earth. There's the sea to go with it!**

AUGUSTE: **Right!** *(AUGUSTE goes after DECORATOR 2. Chase. Eventually, DECORATOR 2 is cornered by lectern.)*

DECORATOR 2: *(Desperately)* **Don't hit me! Remember "Blessed are the merciful for they will be shown mercy."**

AUGUSTE: *(Masking anger)* **All right. I'll let you off, but only because — "Blessed are the pure in heart, for they will see God."**

DECORATOR 1: *(Unctuously)* **And — "Blessed are the peacemakers, for they will be called sons of God."**

AUGUSTE: *(Attempting to resume reading)* **"Blessed are**

189

those **who are persecuted because of righteousness."**

DECORATOR 2: Say that again.

**AUGUSTE: "Blessed are those who are persecuted be-
cause of righteousness."**

DECORATOR 1: You mean you *want* to be persecuted?

AUGUSTE: *(Desperately and unsuccessfully looking for a
way out)* **I . . . I suppose so.**

DECORATOR 1: Well, then, you'll love this. *(As much
business with slosh as possible)*

DECORATOR 2: *(Goes to lectern.)* **"Blessed are those who
are persecuted because of righteousness, for theirs
is the kingdom of heaven." Here ends the lesson.
Come on, we're due at the next job.** *(DECORATORS
collect props and exit.)*

**AUGUSTE: Somehow, I never realized the kingdom of
heaven would be so messy!** *(Exits.)*

190

Ice Cream

*by **Philip Noble***
(Rainbow)

CAST: Two CLOWNS.

PROPS: Sunshade (parasol), foam ball ice cream cone with spring firing mechanism (widely available in toy shops), two small heart-shaped boxes — one in front pocket of each clown, small black rag in CLOWN 2's heart-box, one can of spray-on whipped cream.

OPENING: CLOWN 1 is sitting on bench, center, enjoying a sunny day.

MIME SKETCH: Clown 2 enters with sunshade and large ice cream. *(Some real whipped cream is sprayed generously over the foam ball.)* **He greets Clown 1 politely, sits down next to him/her; then just about to lick cone, offers Clown 1 a lick. Clown 1 refuses.**

   Clown 2 offers a second time. Clown 1 refuses.

   Clown 2 offers, insistently, a third time, and Clown 1 shyly takes the cone. Clown 1 then takes an enormous mouthful, eating all the whipped cream off the top. Enjoys it greatly.

   Clown 2 turns, notices in anger that the whipped cream has gone, and snatches the cone back. He aims, then fires the cone at Clown 1. *(Machine gun background sound is effective here.)*

   Clown 1 collapses.

   Clown 2 realizes what he/she has done. Touches own heart and removes a small heart-shaped box from pocket. He opens the box and pulls out some black, torn material, shows it, then throws it away in contrition. He then turns attention

191

upward, holding the box open, as if to receive blessings from above, closes lid on box and replaces heart.

Clown 2 now approaches Clown 1 and listens for heartbeat. Takes pulse of Clown 1, then opens up Clown 1's heart box *(From front pocket of CLOWN 1's costume)*.

Holding up the open box as before, Clown 2 asks for it to be filled with blessings from above. He then closes box, replaces it, and begins to help Clown 1, who is quickly reviving.

They return to sit on the bench, side by side, sharing the sunshade.

Zack, the Whiz Kid

by *Jim and June Gorgans*
(Rusty and Strawberry)

CAST: Two CLOWNS.

PROPS: Stepladder, binoculars (real or large toy).

Clown 1 comes down aisle, carrying binoculars and dragging ladder, and talking to the audience about having a good seat. He sets up the ladder in the aisle and begins his climb to the top.

Clown 2 enters, asking Clown 1 what he is doing.

Clown 1 tells him that he heard part of the Sunday school story — that this Zack, the Whiz Kid, was going to see Jesus and that he was going to climb a tree to have a good seat.

Clown 2 tells him he misunderstood the story. He then shares with him the story of Zacchaeus, a tax collector who, being short in stature, climbed into a sycamore tree in order to see Jesus. (Luke 19:1-10)

BLOW OFF: Both clowns agree to meet early every Sunday morning for Sunday school, so as not to miss any of the Bible story. As they exit, one invites the other to his house for a Bible study.

Business as (Un)usual

by Janet Litherland

CAST: CLOWN 1 (Storekeeper); CLOWN 2 (Customer).

PROPS: Counter marked "General Store," "Open for Business" sign, a few clown props including stuffed animals, "Closed" sign, feather duster, colorful clown wig, personal clown tricks.

OPENING: CLOWN 1 enters, whistling. Dusts counter and sets out "Open for Business" sign. He then begins to march and practice his tricks. As he plays, he speaks. All "asides" are to the audience. NOTE: CLOWNS must speak distinctly throughout this skit.

CLOWN 1:   Big parade today. And I'm going to be the best clown in it. It's Labor Day, though; so before I go to the parade, I have to "labor" a little — take care of a few customers, do a bit of work. *(Carried away with his antics)* **Boy, wait till the judges see my stuff! I'm pretty good!**

CLOWN 2:   *(Enters and approaches counter. CLOWN 1 jumps behind it and is suddenly "all business.")* **Good morning! I'm going to be in the parade and I want to buy a wig.**

CLOWN 1:   *(Aside)* **Uh, oh. This guy looks good. Too good. Maybe the judges will like him better than me. Methinks me better stifle the competition.**

CLOWN 2:   *(Knocks on counter.)* **Say, there. I said I'm going to be in the parade and I want to buy a wig.**

CLOWN 1:   You want to ride a pig! Sorry, we don't have that sort of thing in this store. *(Aside)* **That ought to fix him!**

CLOWN 2:   No, no! On my *head*. The wig goes on my *head*.

CLOWN 1:   Oh! The pig goes on the *bed*. Why didn't you say so? I have a nice assortment of stuffed animals.

Let's see here . . . *(Looks through merchandise.)*

CLOWN 2: *(Aside)* **This guy's impossible.** *(To CLOWN 1)* **A** *rug!* *(Gestures.)* **A** *head* **rug!**

CLOWN 1: **A bedbug? No, sir! I don't have any stuffed bedbugs.** *(Aside, mockingly)* **Why would anyone want a stuffed bedbug?**

CLOWN 2: **Forget the bedbugs! I want** *hair,* **false hair!**

CLOWN 1: **A waltz chair? Never heard of a waltz chair. I have a nice rocker I'll sell cheap.**

CLOWN 2: **I'll bet you do.** *(Aside)* **He's off** *his* **rocker, that's for sure!** *(Gestures to CLOWN 1.)* **Curls. I want curls all over my head — colorful curls!**

CLOWN 1: **Freshwater pearls. Sure wish I could help you, but business hasn't been good enough for me to stock something that expensive. You know, what with the economy the way it is . . .**

CLOWN 2: **Oh, come on, man — all I want is a** *wig!*

CLOWN 1: *(Aside)* **Now we're back to the pig.** *(To CLOWN 2)* **Looks like I'm not able to help you, sir. What's more, it's time to close. Today's Labor Day, you know. Now that my labors are over, I've got to get ready for the parade.** *(Sets up "Closed" sign.)*

CLOWN 2: **That's why I came in here.** *(Aside)* **All I want is a new wig for the parade. It's a wonder this guy stays in business.** *(Starts to leave.)* **Guess I'll just have to go to a store that's BIG!**

CLOWN 1: **A WIG! Why didn't you say so in the first place? This is a good-looking one.** *(Gets out clown wig and holds it up. CLOWN 2 inspects without touching it.)* **But I can't sell it to you now.**

CLOWN 2: **Why not?**

CLOWN 1: *(Points to sign.)* **I'm closed.**

CLOWN 2: **What?!**

CLOWN 1: **Too bad, too, 'cause this is a nice one. It's** *colorful,* **see?**

195

CLOWN 2: *(Gives audience a knowing look, then speaks to CLOWN 1.)* **You *offer it free?*** *(Snatches wig.)* **Thanks!** *(Exits quickly.)*

CLOWN 1: **Hey! Hey, you!**

CLOWN 2: *(From Off-stage)* **You have a good day, too!**

How to Be a Good Neighbor

by Janet Litherland

CAST: A troupe of CLOWNS.

National Good Neighbor Day was established by presidential proclamation as the fourth Sunday in September. It provides a special opportunity for people to visit the ill, the elderly, and the lonely, and to help those who cannot help themselves. This is a perfect day for clown ministers to really "minister" in a meaningful way.

" 'For I was hungry and you gave me something to eat, I was thirsty and you gave me something to drink, I was a stranger and you invited me in, I needed clothes and you clothed me, I was sick and you looked after me, I was in prison and you came to visit me.' Then the righteous will answer him, 'Lord, when did we see you hungry and feed you, or thirsty and give you something to drink? When did we see you a stranger and invite you in, or needing clothes and clothe you? When did we see you sick or in prison and go to visit you?' The King will reply, 'I tell you the truth, whatever you have done for one of the least of these brothers of mine, you did for me.' " (Matthew 25:35-40, NIV)

Here are some ideas:

Attend church in the morning. Have lunch in the fellowship hall, then put on make-up and costumes. Follow with devotion and prayer for the afternoon's activities. If group is large, send clowns out in pairs or small groups to cover several activities at once. If group is small, select activities and cover them one at a time. Wear or carry signs that say, "This is Good Neighbor Day." And, by all means, take clown props or ideas for no-prop clowning.

1. Get "shut-in" list from pastor and visit those on the list. Offer to help with little chores.

2. Offer to rake someone's yard or cut their grass — free.

3. Have a "Free Car Wash" for an hour or so.

4. Visit the hospital.

5. Visit the nursing home.

6. Visit the prison.

7. In advance, get a list of newcomers from the local Chamber of Commerce or the "Welcome Wagon" and visit them. Entertain them (briefly!) and invite them to attend your church.

8. If your church has an evening service, stay in clown costume and provide refreshments after the service. Be nice to everybody!

COLUMBUS DAY

He Didn't Know
What He Did

by Janet Litherland

CAST: COLUMBUS (a clown), two other male clowns (KINGS), one female clown (QUEEN).

PROPS: Columbus-type hat with plume, three crowns for royalty, beach ball, book, hand-held fan, spring snake, throne (decorated chair).

OPENING: One KING is On-stage, seated on throne.

COLUMBUS: *(Enters, carrying ball. He approaches KING, bowing grandly.)* **Ah, Mr. King, your honor. I mean your highest. Highness! I want to sail the ocean blue in fourteen hundred and ninety-two.**

KING 1: **Fourteen hundred ninety-two what? Ships? Why so many?**

COLUMBUS: **No, the *year* fourteen hundred ninety-two. I'm planning ahead, and I do need ships, but only three.**

KING 1: **Three ships? Why should I give you *any* ships?**

COLUMBUS: **I've been studying and drawing maps.** *(Proudly)* **I'm rather an expert.**

KING 1: **Expert? Aren't you that wool-spinner's kid from down the street? You're no expert! Everyone knows that experts come from out of town.**

COLUMBUS: **Please! I need the ships.**

KING 1: **So go out of town. Ask the King of Portugal. Maybe he'll think you're an expert.** *(Exits, mumbling.)* **Expert! Kids these days!**

COLUMBUS: *(Follows him but does not exit. While his back is turned, next KING enters from opposite side, sits on throne, and opens book. COLUMBUS turns, approaching him. Bowing even lower this time, he falls to his knees.)*

199

Sir! Your Highness! I want to sail around the world.

KING 2: You mean *across* the world. Why?

COLUMBUS: No, sir. *Around* the world. It's round, like this. *(Tosses ball into air and catches it.)* If I start here *(Points to spot on ball)*, I can go around to here, where all the gold is. It's a new route to the East.

KING 2: Oh boy, another nut. Look, sonny. *(Holds out book.)* The world is flat, like *this*. If you sail all the way to the end, you'll fall off, like this! *(Demonstrates by falling off throne.)* That is, provided you don't get eaten up by the dragons that lurk in those unexplored waters. *(Opens shirt to release spring snake.)*

COLUMBUS: *(Snake scares him and he falls back.)* Yeow! *(Recovers.)* Please, sir. I don't really believe in dragons. I need ships.

KING 2: Ships, shmips. *(Rises.)* I'm a king, ring-a-ding-ding, and I say no ships! *(Exits. COLUMBUS follows, shaking his fist and making faces behind his back. He does not exit. While his back is turned, QUEEN enters, sits on throne and begins fanning herself. COLUMBUS turns and approaches her, bowing still lower — prostrates himself.)*

COLUMBUS: Oh, Ma'am, your Beautifulness! Your Greatness! I want to sail on the wind. *(QUEEN shrugs, turns her fan toward him, and fans him vigorously.)* No! That's not what I mean. *(Scrambles to his feet.)* I want to sail the ocean blue in fourteen hundred and ninety-two, but I need ships — three big *galleons*. Will you give them to me? Please, please, please?

QUEEN: What's in it for me?

COLUMBUS: Gold! I'll bring you the gold of the East!

QUEEN: How?

COLUMBUS: By sailing West!

QUEEN: *(Does "take.")* Well, that sounds like a good idea. Makes as much sense as anything my advisors have said all day. *(Rises.)* **Go to the shipyard and tell them Isabella sent you.** *(COLUMBUS jumps for joy, and QUEEN starts to exit.)* **Oh, yes — when you return, you and I will have a little talk.** *(Exits.)*

COLUMBUS: **Wheee! . . . World** *(Holds up ball)*, **I'm going to conquer you!** *(Exits, dribbling the ball.)*

QUEEN: *(Re-enters, calling.)* **Columbus! Hey, Chris! Where are yoooou?** *(COLUMBUS enters dejectedly; beach ball is deflated, too.)* **Oh, there you are! Did you find the gold?**

COLUMBUS: **No, Ma'am, no gold.**

QUEEN: **Well, what *did* you find?**

COLUMBUS: **Nothing really. It was a wasted trip.**

QUEEN: **Oh . . . well, chin up, kid. We all make mistakes.** *(Takes his arm.)*

COLUMBUS: **Oh, I did manage to save you a *little* money.**

QUEEN: **How's that?**

COLUMBUS: *(Grins.)* **I got 12,000 miles to a galleon!**

QUEEN: *(Laughs.)* **Come on, I'll buy you a Pepsi.** *(They exit.)*

201

Deep, Deep as the Ocean

by Janet Litherland

CAST: Two clowns — one FEMALE, one MALE.

PROPS: Two Bibles, paper with writing on both sides.

SETTING: Two tall stools, Center Stage.

OPENING: FEMALE is arranging the stools when MALE enters.

MALE: *(Aside to audience)* **Boy, she's a real beauty! Wonder what it will take to get her attention?** *(To FEMALE)* **Hi! What are you doing?**

FEMALE: **Getting ready for a poetry reading.**

MALE: **Poetry? You mean like "How do I love thee, let me count the days?" Sunday, Monday, Tuesday —**

FEMALE: *(Interrupts.)* **Not *days,* silly — *ways!* "Let me count the *ways.*"**

MALE: **So start counting.** *(Moves quickly toward her.)* **How do you love me?**

FEMALE: **Love *you?* I don't love you. You're funny-looking.**

MALE: **I'm nice, though. Can I be on your program? Can I read poetry with you? Please?**

FEMALE: **Do you have some poetry with you?**

MALE: *(Pulls paper from his pocket.)* **Let's see . . .** *(Reads.)* **"There once was a little toy poodle, who could pick up a pencil and doodle."**

FEMALE: **You've got to be kidding.**

MALE: *(Turns paper over.)* **How about this? "Roses are red, violets are yellow. You'll have to admit, I'm a good-looking fellow."**

FEMALE: **I said you were funny-looking. And your poetry is terrible.**

MALE: What's wrong with it?

FEMALE: It rhymes.

MALE: *(Shocked, he mocks her.)* It *rhymes?* I read a poem that *rhymes?* How sinful of me!

FEMALE: You know what I mean. It's not . . . it's not *deep.*

MALE: Deep? *(Lifts pant legs.)* You're going to wade in *poetry?* *(Aside)* What a dumb way to spend an evening.

FEMALE: Actually, we're going to read deep poetry from the Bible.

MALE: Now you're talking! *(Pulls Bible from pocket.)* When it comes to the Bible, I know about *deep.* *(Quickly turns some pages, then reads.)* Here, listen to this. "Psalms 95:4 — In his hand are the *deep* places of the earth." (KJV) *(Looks into his own hand.)*

FEMALE: Don't be ridiculous.

MALE: I'm supposed to be ridiculous. I'm a clown. *(Flips pages.)* Here's another one. "Job 38:30 — The face of the *deep* is frozen." (KJV) *(Whips his face forward and freezes his position.)*

FEMALE: You're impossible! *(She climbs onto her stool and opens her Bible.)* There *is* deep poetry in the Bible, and it doesn't rhyme. Listen. *(Reads with exaggerated emotion.)* "O ye simple, understand wisdom; and ye *fools* *(Looks at him and he pantomimes, "Who, me?"),* be ye of an understanding heart. *(He pantomimes heart and understanding.)* Hear! *(He cups his ear.)* For I will speak of excellent things. *(He smiles to audience as if to say, "She loves me.")* For wisdom is better than rubies, and all the things that may be desired are not to be compared to it." (Proverbs 8:5-6, 11 KJV) *(He pantomimes "Huh?")*

MALE: *(Aside to audience)* That's a *poem?*

FEMALE: It's from Proverbs.

MALE: You like Proverbs? I like Proverbs. *(Climbs onto other stool and reads.)* **This is a good one. You'll like this one!** *(Mimics her emotional style of reading.)* **"Beauty in a woman without wisdom is like a gold ring in a pig's snout."** (Proverbs 11:22, author's paraphrase.)

FEMALE: *(Swats him and he falls off stool.)* **You have no romance in your soul! You can't read here tonight.**

MALE: **Wait!** *(Scrambles to his feet.)* **Give me another chance. Read something else and I'll try to understand. Please!** *(Aside to audience)* **I can't let her get away. She's just too pretty!**

FEMALE: *(Sighs.)* **OK. Once more.** *(Flips pages and reads, oblivious to anything he does.)* **"Proverbs 24:30-33 — I went by the field of the slothful and by the vineyard of the man void of understanding.** *(MALE turns away and yawns.)* **And, lo, it was all grown over with thorns, and nettles had covered the face thereof, and the stone wall thereof was broken down.** *(MALE sits on floor.)* **Then I saw, and considered it well. I looked upon it, and received instruction.** *(MALE lies down.)* **Yet a little sleep, a little slumber, a little folding of the hands to sleep . . ."** *(KJV. MALE snores loudly.)* **That does it!** *(FEMALE gets off stool, kicks MALE and starts to march off.)*

MALE: *(Rises.)* **What'd I do?** *(Lifts pant legs.)* **I was trying to be *deep*.** *("Wades" around, stepping high.)* **But it just got deeper, and deeper, and deeper, and —**

FEMALE: *(Can't help laughing at him.)* **Oh, come on. I'll teach you. Nobody's hopeless!**

(As she leads him off, he gives big smile to audience and signs, "OK!")

204

National Popcorn Week

National Popcorn Week was established to honor popcorn as a healthy, natural food that is also economical. It is included on most diets these days as a preferred snack. Lucky for us, it tastes good, too!

A popcorn party would be a great way to celebrate this holiday. Since it occurs the same week as Halloween, it could provide a unique alternative, or addition to, Halloween festivities. Keeping children in mind, clowns would be the ideal party-givers, "popping up" with their individual brands of fun throughout the party.

Build around the following party, adapted from *Absolutely Unforgettable Parties* by Janet Litherland, copyright © 1990, Meriwether Publishing Ltd., and conclude with a wonderful Bible lesson developed from a clown's "Stuff Seed" written by Janet Tucker (Jelly Bean).

THE POPCORN PARTY

Gather a group of children in the church fellowship hall or other large room. Decorate with strings of popcorn, corn stalks, and colorful, dried, corn-on-the-cob arrangements. Since the party pops around the corn (pardon the corny pun!), plenty of popcorn is essential. Make plain and buttered popcorn, caramel corn, and miniature popcorn balls.

If you'd like to try flavored popcorn, there are several national distributors that offer such flavors as strawberry, chocolate, coconut, watermelon, peach, jelly-bean, and even bubble gum! Since these could get expensive in quantities, you might give them out sparingly for a "tasting contest," taking a vote to see which flavor the kids like best.

Play a game called "Pop-in" — Divide the group into pairs. Give each person five pieces of popped corn. One pair at a time will try for the most "pop-ins" in the following manner: Facing each other, about six feet apart, one partner tries to pop five pieces of popcorn into his or her partner's mouth; the other partner then does likewise. The number of pieces that fall on the floor are subtracted from 10 for the pair's total score.

The highest scoring pair wins a prize.

Other party suggestions: Relay races involving popcorn and balloons; a good, comedy video with a happy ending. (Always preview videos before showing to a group!)

The Bible story:

A POPCORN STUFF SEED
Based on John 6:1-14

by Janet Tucker
(Jelly Bean)

Put a little popcorn in a popper, then pop it without the lid on (excitement!) as a clown tries to run around catching each piece. Use it to demonstrate the feeding of the 5,000, where a little bit became a lot. Talk about how giving to others out of love — gifts for the needy, visits with shut-ins, phone calls to the lonely — allows God to multiply our gifts.

This "seed" may also be used to show "Give, and it shall be given unto you; good measure, pressed down, and shaken together, and running over . . ." (Luke 6:38, KJV)

Two Activities for
Clown Troupes

by Janet Litherland

CLOWN FESTIVAL

Here is a safe, fun alternative to ghost and goblin activities: Let a troupe of clowns conduct a Clown Festival party for children. Ask all children to dress up as clowns. Teach the children how to juggle and make balloon figures. Play kazoos and let the children parade around the room. Play "Pin the Nose on the Pumpkin." Have a ring toss, a fishing booth, a cupcake walk, a puppet show, storytelling (fun, not frightening), clown skits, and walkarounds. Serve hot dogs, popcorn, shiny red apples, and (of course) candy.

TRICK OR TREAT

Halloween should be a safe, enjoyable time for children. Some people feel this holiday is evil, both in origin and in influence, and should be avoided by church groups altogether. Others see it only as harmless fun, including most children, who don't understand its origin and, in fact, don't even know what "origin" means. Let's lighten up a little and strike a compromise.

Since most children ("churched" and "unchurched") will be trick-or-treating (and they *will*), ensure their safety and their pleasure by organizing them at the church. Clown with them until everyone has arrived, then sit with them and talk about "Allhallowmas" (All Saints' Day) and "Allhallows Eve," which is "Hallows Evening (E'en)" or "Halloween."

Tell them that Halloween started over 2,000 years ago, when people didn't know how the sun and moon worked. They were scared of the dark and believed it was caused by evil spirits. So they built huge bonfires and put on masks to frighten the spirits away. They also gave cakes to the poor in exchange for prayers for a good harvest. These customs went through many changes over the years, mixing with Christian customs, since "Allhallows Eve," the night before All Saints' Day, was a Christian festival. At one time, churches even encouraged people to promote Christianity by joining the street parades on Allhallows Eve, dressed in Bible costumes. Now, we wear all kinds of costumes and go "trick-or-treating" to remind ourselves in a fun way of a time when people didn't understand the universe.

After talking with the children and answering their questions, take them trick-or-treating in mini-groups, one adult clown per group. Before leaving the church, be sure each child is wearing a piece of reflective tape and that each treat bag bears the child's name. Then review the safety rules.

1. Stay with your mini-group.

2. Go only to lighted houses.

3. Don't go inside any houses.

4. Don't walk through yards.

5. Always be polite and say, "Thank you."

6. Clown leaders will each carry a flashlight.

7. Upon returning to church, *all unwrapped, unsealed treats will be discarded.*

Oh, by the way — the "witch" will be the one to tell everyone when it's time to start out. She'll know, because she'll look at her witch watch!

Back at the church: Check each bag for unsealed treats, serve punch or hot cocoa, and clown with the children until their parents pick them up.

Perfect 10

by Kathleen Deegan
(Gracie)

CAST: Four or more CLOWNS, one of whom can do simple gymnastics such as cartwheels, round offs, and splits.

PROPS: Sheets of construction paper with a large "10" written on each sheet — one per clown; poster that reads "In God's Eyes We Can All Be Perfect 10s."

MIME SKETCH: The "judges" *(All clowns except performing clown)* enter and go to front of audience, keeping construction paper at sides with "10" hidden.

Performing clown enters and does a couple of cartwheels, round offs, splits, as if in competition. When finished with routine, performer exits.

Each judge, one at a time, holds up his or her number "10" for audience to see. *(Plant someone to start applause for each judge's decision.)*

When all judges have shown their scores, performing clown walks to front of audience and displays the poster.

ALL SAINTS' DAY

The Imperfect Saint

by Janet Litherland

CAST: Two CLOWNS.

PROPS: Feather duster, piece of sandpaper, loop of paper that can be worn over clown costumes like a beauty pageant banner is worn — says, "Saint Joey" (Use CLOWN 2's own name.)

OPENING: CLOWN 2 sits, center, sanding the handle of his feather duster.

CLOWN 1: *(Enters, carrying the paper banner.)* **Hey! Did you hear what the preacher said this morning about sainthood?**

CLOWN 2: **Wasn't there. I was busy fixing my feather duster.**

CLOWN 1: **What's wrong with it?**

CLOWN 2: **Nothing, now. The handle was broken.**

CLOWN 1: **Let's see.** *(Examines it.)* **Looks pretty good to me. Can't even see where it broke.**

CLOWN 2: **Oh, the crack's still there, but I patched it with Super Glue and sanded it.** *(Admires work.)* **Then I painted it and sanded it again. You can't see where it's broken, but I still know it's broken ... So what did the preacher say?**

CLOWN 1: **He said we're *all* called to be saints, every one of us. So I had this banner made especially for you because you're my friend.** *(Drapes it across CLOWN 2's body.)* **Whatcha think?**

CLOWN 2: **Saint Joey? I think you got it all wrong, Nikky.** *(Use CLOWN 1's own name.)* **I'm no saint!**

CLOWN 1: **Listen to this. The preacher said there are three requirements for sainthood.** *(Numbers them on his fingers.)* **Belong to God — you do. Believe in Jesus**

Christ as Lord and Savior — you do. And be filled
with the Holy Spirit — you are. Therefore, you're a
saint. Let's celebrate!

CLOWN 2:   No, Nikky. Saints are supposed to be perfect. I'm flawed.

CLOWN 1:   Flawed? Whatcha mean you're flawed?

CLOWN 2:   I've got cracks in my character. Think about
it — haven't I been resentful sometimes? *(CLOWN 1
nods reluctantly.)* A little jealous, especially when
Jumbo was looking at my sweet Millie? *(CLOWN 1
nods.)* Even shown some temper once in a while?
(Nods.)

CLOWN 1:   OK, so you're flawed. You can still be a saint.

CLOWN 2:   How do you figure?

CLOWN 1:   Well, it's like your broken feather duster.
It's patched so you can't tell it was ever broken, and
it will work real good for a long, long time. Same
with you. God patched you up pretty good, and
you'll be good for a long, long time.

CLOWN 2:   *(Stands.)* But *I* still know the feather duster's
broken.

CLOWN 1:   God still knows you're broken, too, but he
wants you anyway. It's OK to be patched.

CLOWN 2:   So what about you? Are you a saint, too?

CLOWN 1:   *(Sits on bench.)* I'm working on it. I'm learning
the "blessed are's" and trying to be like them. "Blessed are the meek ... blessed are the merciful ..."

CLOWN 2:   Hmmmm ... Want some help?

CLOWN 1:   Sure!

CLOWN 2:   "Blessed are ye ... when men shall *perse-
cute* you ... *(Begins to tickle CLOWN 1 with feather duster)* for my sake ... for great is your reward in
heaven!" (Matthew 5:11, 12; KJV) *(CLOWN 1 giggles,
laughs, jumps up, and runs off, giggling and being tickled
all the way.)*

211

Election Day Coverage

by Janet Litherland

This is the day to encourage people to vote (but not for a particular person or party). It is definitely a "service" worthy of clown ministers, and what better way to attract attention than with clowns!

Get permission from the police department, then work streets and shopping malls. With planning and advance advertising, a clown troupe could provide rides to the polls for retirement home residents, homebound mothers, and others who might not have transportation.

Wear big "Go Vote!" signs, front or back, or sticking up out of a hat, and let each clown do his or her own brand of clown funny business. If anyone asks a clown *how* he votes, he can always say, "Republicrat," or "Demopublican!"

THANKSGIVING
What's It All About?

by Janet Litherland

CAST: Three clowns — MOTHER, FATHER, CHILD.

PROPS: Bibles on table, juggling balls and kazoo for child.

SETTING: Living room — table, sofa, chair, hassock.

OPENING: FATHER and CHILD are seated; MOTHER is Off-stage.

MOTHER: *(Enters.)* **Well, Aunt Elvira just called. She's coming for Thanksgiving, too. That makes eighteen people! What are we going to** *do?*

FATHER: **Eat turkey, of course.**

CHILD: **Isn't that what Thanksgiving is all about?**

MOTHER: **I'm not sure. I'm sorry we can't ask Uncle Henry, too, but they're divorced. That would just make one more anyway, and we're running out of room.**

CHILD: **Why** *can't* **we have Uncle Henry for dinner?**

FATHER: **We can, but turkey tastes better!** *(CHILD laughs.)* **That reminds me — do you know what the electric mixer said to the turkey?**

CHILD: **No, what?**

FATHER: **I can beat the stuffing out of you!** *(CHILD really laughs.)*

MOTHER: **Come on, you two. What are we going to do with so many people all day?**

FATHER: **Well, we can put our dinner on trays and bring them in here, and watch football on TV.** *(Puts feet up on hassock and gets comfortable.)* **Isn't that what Thanksgiving is all about?**

MOTHER: *(Whacks him out of his seat.)* **I don't think so.**

CHILD: **I know!** *(Rises.)* **We can go downtown and see**

the Thanksgiving Day Parade. We can even be *in* it. *(Starts juggling.)* Maybe that's what Thanksgiving is all about. Santa Claus will be there too!

MOTHER: Santa Claus! *(Snatches one of the balls out of the air and others fall.)* I don't think Thanksgiving is about Santa Claus.

FATHER: *(Still on floor, sitting up now.)* Well, do you have any ideas?

MOTHER: I was thinking we might all go to the Thanksgiving service at church. *(Sits near table.)*

CHILD: Church! On *Thanksgiving?*

MOTHER: Isn't that what Thanksgiving is all about? Giving thanks? *(Picks up Bible.)* Listen to what I read this morning in Psalms: "It is a good thing to give thanks to the Lord, and to sing praises to his name. To show forth his loving kindness in the morning, and his faithfulness every night, with stringed instruments and the harp . . ." *(To CHILD)* I think he might even like a little praise from your kazoo. *(Resumes reading.)* "For you have made me glad, Lord. I will sing for joy because of all the wonderful things you have done." (Psalm 92:1-4; author's paraphrase)

CHILD: Gee, I never thought of it that way.

MOTHER: Then I guess that's my fault. Too much attention to dinner.

FATHER: And football.

CHILD: And parades?

MOTHER: And parades. We've got a lot to be thankful for — freedom, hope, love . . . and our family, all eighteen of them. Let's take them to church, and *then* we'll eat dinner. *(Rises.)*

FATHER: *(Scrambles to feet.)* And maybe watch just a *little* football? *(Fakes a pass.)*

MOTHER: *(Smiles.)* A little.

CHILD: And see a little of the parade? *(Marches in*

214

place . . . Pauses, as MOTHER fixes a "look" on him/her.)
. . . Except for Santa Claus.

MOTHER: *(Laughs.)* **Except for Santa Claus. He's out of season.**

(All three march off singing "Come, Ye Thankful People, Come." [Page 694 in The United Methodist Hymnal *— may be found in most hymnals.] CHILD sings through his/her kazoo.)*

215

Preparations

by Janet Litherland

CAST: Two CLOWNS.

PROPS: Two clown telescopes, pair of huge glasses, broom.

SETTING: Broom is propped against wall, left.

OPENING: CLOWN 1 sits on edge of stage, center, with telescope, scanning the sky. CLOWN 2 enters left, crossing stage.

CLOWN 2:   **Come on, let's go to the party. They're having pony rides.**

CLOWN 1:   **I'm busy.**

CLOWN 2:   *(Stops.)* **Too busy for a party?** *(Peers at telescope.)* **What's that thing?**

CLOWN 1:   **A telescope.**

CLOWN 2:   *(Indicates to audience that it looks weird, but he doesn't say so.)* **Sure it is. What's it for?**

CLOWN 1:   **To see things that are a long ways away.**

CLOWN 2:   **Can I see?**

CLOWN 1:   **Sure, I've got another one.** *(Hands CLOWN 2, who remains standing, the other telescope.)*

CLOWN 2:   *(Looks through it.)* **Just stars and stuff. They're still a long ways away. What's so interesting?**

CLOWN 1:   **The preacher said this is Advent, the time when everyone should look for the Messiah.**

CLOWN 2:   *(Flabbergasted)* **The Messiah! You're looking for the Messiah ... up** *there?*

CLOWN 1:   **Yep. The Bible says, "The glory of the Lord shall be revealed, and all flesh shall see it together ..."** (Isaiah 40:5, KJV) **That's us — "flesh."** *(Pinches self, then pinches leg of CLOWN 2 who yelps and grabs his leg.)* **Flesh!** *(Does both pinches again.)*

CLOWN 2: Ooow! Quit that!

CLOWN 1: The Bible says —

CLOWN 2: I know what it says. *(Sits beside CLOWN 1.)* Listen, I don't think it means use a telescope.

CLOWN 1: *(Puts telescope down and puts on clown glasses.)* I tried my glasses, but they didn't work. Do you have binoculars with you?

CLOWN 2: No.

CLOWN 1: A magnifying glass?

CLOWN 2: No! That's not what the Scripture means.

CLOWN 1: How else can I look for him?

CLOWN 2: You don't look *for* him, Joey. *(Use CLOWN's own name.)* You look *forward* to his coming. That's what Advent means.

CLOWN 1: *(As a revelation)* Ohh! Look forward to Christmas? *(CLOWN 2 nods.)* Well, I guess I can do that pretty well.

CLOWN 2: Sure you can. Advent is a wonderful time. You can also go to the party with me. Let's go! *(Gets up.)*

CLOWN 1: Is "looking forward" easier than just "looking"?

CLOWN 2: Not really. But it makes more sense. *(Starts Off Right. CLOWN 1 starts left.)* Where are you going? The party's this way!

CLOWN 1: I'm coming, I'm coming. *(Grabs broom and starts moving right, backwards, sweeping the path in front of his body as he goes. He passes CLOWN 2.)*

CLOWN 2: What are you *doing?*

CLOWN 1: *(Continues.)* The Bible says, "Prepare ye the way of the Lord . . ." (Matthew 3:3, KJV) *(Exits backwards, sweeping.)*

CLOWN 2: You just don't get it, do you? *(Runs Off Right, after him.)*

217

Mary's Baby Shower

by Trudy Cravatta-DiNardo
(Sparky)

NOTE FROM TRUDY: The idea for this skit came from a fellow clown, David W. Lloyd (see page 27). I wrote it and directed it for the Sunday school of First Presbyterian Church in Allentown, Pennsylvania. Performers were clowns from First Presbyterian Church and clowns from The Sunshine Troupe of Upper Bucks County. The skit takes 20 minutes; rhythm and timing are important.

CAST: Two PUPPETEERS (not clowns) dressed in black, MARY (woman — not a clown — in Bible costume), troupe of CLOWNS.

PROPS: Two puppets, banner — "Baby Shower" taped on puppets' lectern, party items — balloons, noisemakers, etc., colorful watering can, ornate umbrella, one comfortable chair Down Right, *oversized* shower gifts — baby bottle, diaper and pins, pacifier, rattle, crayon and coloring book, card with many signatures, clock, inflated heart; also, a long balloon, baby buggy, and real Advent wreath.

SETTING: Puppeteers work on podium at Down Left side of chancel area or stage.

OPENING: PUPPET 1 enters, humming, carrying party items. PUPPET 2 enters and watches PUPPET 1. PUPPET 1 turns and bumps into PUPPET 2.

PUPPET 2:   **What's goin' on? What are you doin'?**

PUPPET 1:   **I'm getting ready for a shower!**

PUPPET 2:   **Are you dirty?**

PUPPET 1:   **No.**

PUPPET 2:   **A shower? Is it going to rain?**

PUPPET 1:   **I don't think so.**

PUPPET 2:   **What shower? What are you talking about?**

PUPPET 1:   *(Realizes the confusion and giggles.)* **Oh, how silly of me! I'm getting ready for a baby shower!**

PUPPET 2: *(Looking up, shocked)* **Oh, my, is it going to rain babies from the sky?**

PUPPET 1: *(Laughs.)* **Oh, no. A baby shower isn't babies falling from the sky. A baby shower is a kind of party, usually given to a woman who is going to have a baby. People bring the woman gifts for her unborn baby.**

PUPPET 2: **Who is the woman that is going to have a baby?**

PUPPET 1: **The Virgin Mary. A bunch of us are going to give Mary a baby shower.**

PUPPET 2: **May I help?**

PUPPET 1: **Sure. As a matter of fact, here she comes! Look!**

(Christmas music begins. "Greensleeves" is suggested. MARY enters from back of room and is escorted by two CLOWNS. One CLOWN is in front of MARY, carrying watering can; the other is behind MARY, holding umbrella over her head. As MARY arrives Down Center, CLOWNS take places right and left of her.)

PUPPET 2: **Hi, Mary!**

PUPPET 1: **Are you surprised?**

MARY: **Yes!**

PUPPET 2: **Hey guys, make Mary comfortable in that nice chair over there.**

(MARY moves to chair. CLOWNS sits on floor, one on each side of MARY.)

PUPPET 1: **Mary, we would like to present to you some special gifts for your unborn baby, our Savior. Oh, Mary, who's going to take care of your gift list?**

(CLOWN in congregation raises hand, then moves to MARY's right.)

PUPPET 2:   For your hungry baby, here's a bottle.

(CLOWN in congregation rises, holding BIG bottle. He eagerly skips to MARY and presents her with gift — CLOWN on her right takes gift and places it near MARY. Each new CLOWN sits on alternating sides of MARY. Keep MARY on the highest level and the CLOWNS below her. Same stage directions apply throughout the presentation of gifts.)

PUPPET 1:   To help keep the baby dry, here's a diaper and pins.

PUPPET 2:   If the baby cries, here's a pacifier.

PUPPET 1:   We thought the baby would like a nice toy, so here's a rattle.

PUPPET 2:   So the baby can color, here's a crayon and a coloring book.

PUPPET 1:   So you can take the baby for a breath of fresh air, here's a baby buggy.

(PUPPET 1 whispers to PUPPET 2.)

PUPPET 2:   And here's a card from all of us . . . so you can remember this special baby shower. *(CLOWN may hang oversized card in visible place.)*

(If your congregation is conducting a toy drive for a special group, the following procession would allow them to participate in this skit. If not, eliminate the procession and continue with PUPPET 2.)

PUPPET 1:   Mary, the people of *(Your church)* **have Christmas gifts for the** *(Name of charity).* **May they please bring their gifts now?**

(MARY nods, and procession follows. CLOWNS help people to arrange gifts all around the altar or in a specified place. After the procession, a few CLOWNS move Down Center, then start to exit. They have no gifts.)

PUPPET 2: Hey, where are you guys going? *(CLOWNS stop and look at PUPPETS, shrugging shoulders.)*

PUPPET 1: Wait! You *do* have many gifts you can give the unborn Savior. *(CLOWN closest to PUPPETS moves to them.)* **One gift is your** *time. (PUPPET lifts BIG clock.)* **You can give the Christ Child your time by spending time with your parents, friends, and one another.** *(PUPPET gives clock to CLOWN; CLOWN presents it to MARY.)*

PUPPET 2: There's another gift you can give the Messiah. *(Second CLOWN moves to PUPPETS.)* **You can give him your** *love. (PUPPET lifts inflated, or red cardboard, heart.)* **You can give him your love by praying to him and keeping his commandments.** *(PUPPET gives heart to CLOWN; CLOWN presents it to MARY.)*

PUPPET 1: Still another gift *(Motions for third CLOWN to approach)* **is giving the Baby Jesus your gentle** *touch* **by kissing, hugging, and holding hands with one another.**

(CLOWN thinks a moment and moves to MARY. He takes a long balloon out of his pocket, blows it up and makes a cross out of it. Gives it to MARY and kneels. MARY rises and cradles cross as if cross is a baby. Music begins — "By Your Touch" by Jaime Rickert is suggested. ["By Your Touch" is available on cassette, Jaime Rickert of the Parish Mission Team, *copyright © 1986, J. W. Rickert. Contact Parish Mission Team, 38 Montebello Road, Suffern, NY 10901.] MARY moves to Advent wreath, raises balloon cross, and places it in center of wreath. She turns, and CLOWNS gather around her. They exit to the music.)*

CHRISTMAS

The 20th Century
Mystery Play

Based on Luke 2:1-19 and Matthew 2:1-10

by David W. Lloyd (Cop a Plea and Poppatui) **and the
Faith and Fantasy Group of the Seekers Faith
Community of the Church of the Saviour**

CAST: NARRATOR, a "SIGN" CLOWN (holds up signs),
several other CLOWNS (all silent).

PROPS: Signs — Social Security, Holiday Inn, Stable, Sore,
Reggie Jackson, Sheep (2 or 3), Star, Bethlehem. Wellspring, Field, Afraid, Jerusalem, King of the Juice. A number
for each clown (use stick-on name tags), offering plates,
kazoos for several clowns, four animal masks — donkey,
cow, chicken, sheep; can of "Behold" furniture polish, box
of "Glad" bags, box of "Tide" detergent, bottle of "Joy"
dish detergent, three gifts for wise persons, apple.

NARRATOR: This year, we thought and thought about
what we could do that would be new and different,
and we decided on a Christmas pageant! Only we
were tired of all the solemnity that usually is part
of the whole thing, so we decided to look at the
Christmas story with fresh eyes to see the comedy
that underlies God's incarnation as Jesus. We want
to tell the story the way it "really" happened.

Only we don't have enough clowns, so we will
need your help at various places to fill the roles. I'm
going to be the Narrator, and we hope you will join
in as "The Heavenly Host" whenever we add music.

And now, on to "The 20th Century Mystery
Play."

*(All CLOWNS enter, walk around. NARRATOR pauses
each time CLOWNS have action.)*

As you know, the story begins: "Now in the days

of Caesar Augustus, a decree went out that all the world should be taxed." To start with, this meant there had to be a census, which means everyone had to get a Social Security number *(SIGN CLOWN posts "Social Security" sign)* and then they could collect the tax. *(All CLOWNS get "number" from SIGN CLOWN.)* Or tithes and offerings, if you prefer. *(Two CLOWNS collect offering.)*

Now, some people had to go to their ancestral home. *(CLOWNS search for home.)* Since Judea and Galilee hadn't ratified the ERA, that meant the home of the paternal ancestor. *(SIGN CLOWN posts "Bethlehem" sign.)* That's how Joseph and his fiancee, Mary, came to be traveling to Bethlehem. *(CLOWNS kazoo "O Little Town of Bethlehem" and encourage audience to join in humming. One CLOWN becomes INN-KEEPER.)*

Now Joseph was no dummy, and he noticed that Mary was getting, well, uh, a little plump! So when they got to Bethlehem, Joseph didn't waste any time in getting to the Holiday Inn, *(SIGN CLOWN posts "Holiday Inn")* where he had called ahead for reservations. Holiday Inn? *(One CLOWN nods vigorously.)* Oh, I get it — a "holiday" inn, because it was **Christmas**. *(CLOWN nods with satisfaction.)*

But the innkeeper informed them that the tenants had taken a vote the previous week and had opted for condominium conversion — hey! Wait a minute, what is this? — and so no rooms were available.

Joseph let his fingers do the walking to find another place, but there was a Wellspring *(SIGN CLOWN posts "Wellspring")* orientation that week, so none of the other hotels and boarding homes had rooms either. But the innkeeper, seeing the delicate circumstances, agreed to let them sleep in the parking garage. *(Two CLOWNS disagree.)* **The sauna?** *(Disagree)* **The riding stable?** *(Sort of disagree)* **The stable.** *(They agree, and SIGN CLOWN posts "Stable.")*

But they weren't alone in the stable. Besides the horses, there was Joseph's donkey, a cow, a chicken, and a sheep. *(Some CLOWNS kazoo "The Friendly Beasts" [May be found in* Tomie dePaola's Book of Christmas Carols, New York: G. P. Putnam's Sons, *copyright © 1987, among other sources] as other CLOWNS select members of congregation to be animals and help them put on masks.)* **There wasn't a pig, though, because the pig was doing the narration.** *Now wait a minute!* **That line just isn't kosher.**

Meanwhile, out in left field, no, right field, no, center field were some shepherds. *(SIGN CLOWN posts "Field" and three CLOWNS stand under sign. One CLOWN recruits a member of congregation to be ANGEL and takes him/her out for costuming.)* **Where there are shepherds, there are bound to be sheep.** *(CLOWNS recruit a few more SHEEP and SIGN CLOWN gives them "Sheep" signs.)* **These shepherds used to brag about their sheep. Yes, they did. They used to say they were outstanding in their field. C'mon, sheep, let me see you smile.** *That's* **what I call a sheepish grin.**

(CLOWN enters with ANGEL.) **Moving right along ... And lo, an angel appeared unto them.** *(NARRATOR scolds CLOWNS.)* **What's the matter? Haven't you heard of the "Herald" Angel sings?** *(CLOWNS kazoo "Hark, the Herald Angels Sing.")*

Oh, I forgot to introduce the shepherds. The shepherds were *(SIGN CLOWN gives signs to three SHEPHERDS.)* **"Sore," "Afraid," and in right field, wearing number forty-four, "Reggie Jackson."**

The angel said, "Fear not! For behold! *(CLOWN*

gives can of "Behold" to ANGEL.) **I bring you glad** *(Gives box of "Glad" bags)* **tidings** *(Gives box of "Tide" detergent)* **of great joy.** *(Gives "Joy" bottle.)* **I feel like I'm doing a commercial for a soap opera!** *(At this time, a CLOWN recruits a member of congregation as BABY JESUS and takes him out for costuming. Another recruits the STAR and takes him/her for costume, telling him/her to bow whenever NARRATOR says STAR. Still another recruits three WISE PERSONS and takes them for costumes.)*

For unto you is born this day in the city of brotherly love — well, wasn't this Bethlehem, Pennsylvania? OK, in the city of David, a Savior who is Christ the Lord. And this shall be a sign unto you. You shall find him, or her, wrapped in swaddling clothes and telling lies in the manger. *(Two CLOWNS disagree.)* **Oh, *lying* in the manger.** *(They agree.)*

So the shepherds and their outstanding sheep went to Bethlehem *(SHEPHERDS guide sheep to stable area, and BABY JESUS is brought in)* **and found Mary, Joseph, and the Baby already standing up in the crib.** *(CLOWNS kazoo "Away in a Manger.")*

At the same time, there were wise persons in the east who had observed a new star. *(STAR is brought in and bows.)* **Let's hear it for the star** *(Bows)* **of our show!** *(Applause)*

They followed the star *(Bows)* **to Jerusalem.** *(SIGN CLOWN posts "Jerusalem" and WISE PERSONS enter with gifts.)* **There they met Herod the Grape.** *(One CLOWN takes role of HEROD.)* **They asked him, "Where is this King of the Juice?** *(SIGN CLOWN posts "King of the Juice.")* **We have observed his star** *(Bows)* **in the east."**

King Herod thought he was a big apple *(HEROD displays apple and snatches the King sign)* **and King of**

the Juice, and got rather upset by this — sour grapes — so he called the wise persons to him and questioned them about the star *(Bows)* they were following. They said it was O. J. Simpson — O. J., orange juice, get it?

He told them to go to Bethlehem, find this grape new king, and to come back to tell him so that he could worship him too. They promised not to "welch" on the grape king. *(CLOWNS kazoo "We Three Kings," as WISE PERSONS go to Bethlehem.)*

When they arrived in the vicinity of the stable, they wished they had brought gas masks — all those smelly animals. Then they had to zigzag through the barnyard, because back in those days the EPA didn't have emissions under control. Finally, they found Mary, Joseph, the shepherds, moderators, pastor-prophets, the baby — no longer lie-ing, only mildly exaggerating — assorted animals, Noah. No, wait! That's another story.

They fell down and worshiped, and brought gifts. First, gold, including tithes and offerings. *(Gifts presented.)* Then frankincense, which is incense used in worship services. *(Presented)* Then myrrh, which is really a perfume for embalming.*(Presented)*

(CLOWNS kazoo "Silent Night.") This concludes our irreverent look at the Christmas story. But the scriptural account is just as strange. As I read the biblical account of the story, we'd like you to reflect upon it — in awe, in wonder, and in reverence. *(CLOWNS and CONGREGATION PARTICIPANTS remain at stable until Scripture concludes. NARRATOR reads Luke 2:1-19 and Matthew 2:1-10.)*

God Is . . .

by Philip Noble
(Rainbow)

CAST: Twelve CLOWNS, one CONDUCTOR CLOWN.

PROPS: One of the following big-letter cards for each clown — D, E, E, G, H, I, N, O, O, R, S, W. Baton for Conductor.

MIME SKETCH: Clowns enter, each carrying a letter. They look at one another, then begin arranging themselves into phrases such as WE SHINER GOOD, GO REWIND HOSE, RED SHOE OWING, and other variations.

   Conductor enters grandly. He assembles the clowns in the "correct" order, then turns to the audience to take a bow.

   In mid-bow, he notices that the message reads: GOD IS NOWHERE. He returns to gently push the clown with the H away from the clown with the W.

   Conductor turns and bows.

   The message reads:

Variations: JESUS IS NOW HERE (14 clowns)

   THE MESSIAH IS NOW HERE (19 clowns)

CHAPTER FIVE

SKITS FOR CLOWNING AROUND

Other Days

The skits in this chapter were written by the clown ministers, not for special days, but for special reasons or effects. "Paul in Prison," for example, grew out of Stephen Ashcroft's burden for prison ministry. It's a way to "connect" with prisoners so that ministry can begin.

J. T. Sikes had drug abuse in mind when he wrote, "Things Aren't Always What They Seem"; "The Dancing Clown" was a natural transition for Olive Drane, who is a dancer and has a great interest in dance-worship; and Mark Seckel's "A Little Sin Is Too Much" may have been designed to teach a Bible concept, but it is clearly calculated to keep children bubbling with giggles as bright and frothy as the soap suds that bubble out of the clown's mixing bowl!

Open your heart to these special skits — they can be special to your ministry, too!

Paul in Prison

Based loosely on Philippians 1

by Stephen Ashcroft
(Ludo the Clown)

CAST: Two clowns — WHITEFACE as St. Paul, AUGUSTE.

PROPS: Pen, huge roll of paper, large sack containing packet of spaghetti, knitting needles, chicken costume, teaspoon, two tiny flower pots, trumpet.

OPENING: WHITEFACE enters with pen and roll of paper and begins writing.

WHITEFACE: **Dear Philippians . . . This is your old pal, Paul. Hope this finds you as it leaves me. I am in prison at the moment . . .**

(AUGUSTE enters with large sack. He creeps up behind WHITEFACE and shouts, "Boo!" WHITEFACE screams.)

WHITEFACE: **Why, it's you. I was just writing to you and the other Philippians. Have you come all this way to visit me?**

AUGUSTE: **Yes. And isn't it a business getting in here?** *(Goes into long speech about going through doors, up stairs, through another door, along corridors, around corners, etc. WHITEFACE ties his arms in knots, trying to trace route with hands. Eventually interrupts.)*

WHITEFACE: **Well, you're here now.**

AUGUSTE: **Yes, and I've brought you something.** *(Indicates sack.)*

WHITEFACE: **For me? How did you smuggle it in?**

AUGUSTE: **I can't tell you. It's too embarrassing.**

WHITEFACE: **What's in it?**

AUGUSTE: *(With exaggerated secrecy)* **An escape kit. Here.** *(Gives WHITEFACE packet of spaghetti.)*

WHITEFACE: **Spaghetti? How do I escape with this?**

AUGUSTE: **With these.** *(Hands out knitting needles.)* **You**

cook the spaghetti and knit it into a rope ladder. Then, when you've climbed down it, you eat the ladder and no one knows where you've gone!

WHITEFACE: *(Heavy with sarcasm)* **Thank you.**

AUGUSTE: **You don't like the idea.**

WHITEFACE: **Not a lot.**

AUGUSTE: **Then how about this?**

WHITEFACE: *(Sees what AUGUSTE is holding and recoils.)* **A chicken costume!**

AUGUSTE: **Yes! You put it on and stand in the corner of your cell going, "Cluck, cluck, cluck."** *(WHITEFACE and AUGUSTE do chicken impressions.)* **Then when the wardens come, they think, "Oh, there's only a chicken in here. Paul must have escaped. We'd better go and find him." Then, while they're looking for you, you walk out and escape.**

WHITEFACE: **Thank you.**

AUGUSTE: **You don't like it. Never mind, I've got another idea.**

WHITEFACE: **I was afraid of that.**

AUGUSTE: **Here!** *(Gives WHITEFACE a teaspoon.)*

WHITEFACE: **Don't tell me — this is to dig a tunnel.**

AUGUSTE: **That's right.**

WHITEFACE: *(Reacts. He thought AUGUSTE had been joking.)* **What do I do with the earth?**

AUGUSTE: **You put it in these.** *(Offers two tiny flower pots.)*

WHITEFACE: **They'll get full.**

AUGUSTE: **Then you empty them out the window.**

WHITEFACE: **But by the time I've dug the tunnel, there'll be enough earth outside the window for me to climb down and escape that way.**

AUGUSTE: **Exactly! You'll confuse 'em. They won't know which way you've gone!**

231

WHITEFACE: Anyway, they'll hear me digging.

AUGUSTE: Not if you play this. *(Hands out trumpet.)*

WHITEFACE: Let me get this straight. Your idea is that I should make a rope ladder out of spaghetti, or, if that doesn't work, I should dig a tunnel with a teaspoon and escape wearing a chicken costume and playing a trumpet. *(Trumpet blast in AUGUSTE's ear)* Is that right?

AUGUSTE: Do you think it will work?

WHITEFACE: *(Slow burn, then controls himself.)* I don't think I want to escape. *(Indicates chicken costume.)* Something tells me I'm not meant to.

AUGUSTE: *(Downcast)* But ... but we've put so much work into this. Everyone in Philippi collected to buy the things, and Mrs. Epaphroditus spent weeks making the chicken costume, and I've come all this way, and ... *(Trails off in tears.)*

WHITEFACE: And you've brought me the one thing I needed.

AUGUSTE: *(Half cheered)* The chicken costume?

WHITEFACE: No, not the chicken costume. I needed to know that there are people out there who remember me, and think about me, and pray for me. And you've shown me that's true. That's all I need to be happy.

AUGUSTE: Oh ... well ... that's all right then. I suppose I'd better take these things away with me.

WHITEFACE: *(With fervor)* Yes, please. *(They stuff things back into sack, and AUGUSTE starts to go.)* Hey! You couldn't smuggle this letter out for me, could you? *(Indicates roll of paper.)*

AUGUSTE: Where could I hide that?

WHITEFACE: I'm too embarrassed to tell you.

AUGUSTE: All right, then. *(Takes roll.)* Bye! *(Exits.)*

WHITEFACE: *(To AUGUSTE)* **Bye!** *(To audience)* **Bye!**

NOTE FROM STEPHEN: This sketch has been success-fully performed in several prisons.

Testimony Food

by Randy Christensen

CAST: One CLOWN.

PROPS: Kix (cereal), Off (insect repellent), Coast (bar soap), Scope (mouthwash), Dawn (dishwashing soap), All (laundry detergent), Just Right (cereal), Wisk (laundry detergent), Renew (recyclable trash bags), Zest (bar soap), Joy (dishwashing soap), Life (cereal), Vanish (toilet bowl cleaner), Mr. Clean (household cleanser), Brite, Future (floor wax), Sunlight (dishwashing soap), Resolve (carpet cleaner), Baby Fresh (baby wipes), Lifebuoy (bar soap), Secret (deodorant), Nut 'n Honey (cereal).

OPENING: CLOWN enters, carrying bags of groceries, apologizing for being late. (Purchase the brands listed and pull them from the bags when calling out their names.)

CLOWN: You know, my mind kind of wanders when I think of all that Jesus has done for me! Often when I grocery shop, I see that food for the body, and I begin to think about "food for the soul." I lose track of time!

Some folks may really get their KIX out of my grocery shopping. When I shop, I walk the aisles and think about the changes Jesus has made in my heart and home.

I usually take a shopping list, but when I start thinking about the Lord, I get distracted and seem to get a bit OFF.

I grew up fairly religious, but I was pretty much just COAST-ing along. I didn't realize the SCOPE of my predicament due to sin. Then it DAWNed on me . . .

I needed to give my ALL to Jesus. Without him, life could never be JUST RIGHT. Well, when I did, he WISKed my sins away, RENEWed my ZEST for living, and brought new JOY into my LIFE. My sin VANISHed. Now, I feel like MR. CLEAN!

Because of him, I have a BRITE FUTURE. There's SUNLIGHT in my soul. I have a new RE-SOLVE. I feel BABY FRESH. It's a great LIFEBUOY!

It's no SECRET, without Jesus . . . you ain't got NUT 'N HONEY!

The Banana Illusion
(Our Christian version)

by Rafael Rondon and Carlos Sanchez
((Bombin & Archie)

NOTE: This skit could be adapted for April Fool's Day.

CAST: Two CLOWNS.

PROPS: A banana, a plastic bag hidden in the pocket of Clown B, a yellow handkerchief about 12" x 12". (To fold handkerchief for this skit, grab it in the middle and bring the four corners up.)

CLOWN A: *(Enters and speaks to audience.)* **Ladies and gentlemen, you are now going to see one of the greatest illusions of the world!**

(CLOWN B enters without CLOWN A's knowledge. He stands, listening, curious.)

CLOWN A: **And for this illusion we need a banana.**

(CLOWN B hears this, is excited about it, and leaves stage to look for his banana. While he is gone, CLOWN A explains.)

CLOWN A: **But this is not a real banana. It is a yellow handkerchief** *representing* **a banana!** *(Pulls out handkerchief as CLOWN B re-enters with real banana.)* **And now, The Banana Illusion!**

(CLOWN B stands beside CLOWN A.

(Audience)

236

They are in a "V" formation, both playing to the audience, but not to each other.)

CLOWN A: **To begin, we peel the banana open in four places. One** . . . *(He peels one strip.)* **Two** . . . **three** . . . **and four.** *(All four corners are "peeled." At the same time, CLOWN B peels his real banana in the same manner.)* **The banana is open now!**

(CLOWN B starts like he is going to eat his, but is stopped by CLOWN A's words.)

CLOWN A: **And now! We are going to close the banana.**

(CLOWN B reacts as if this is very strange, but he keeps going with CLOWN A. From this point, CLOWN B reacts with funny faces and no comments.)

CLOWN A: *(Begins closing the banana.)* **One** . . . **two** . . . **three** . . . **and four.** *(CLOWN B does same.)* **And now we are going to fold the banana in half!** *(CLOWN B reacts with gestures of "Ughh, yukk," etc., but he manages to fold his banana.)* **And now, we fold it in half again.** *(CLOWN A now has a neatly folded handkerchief, and CLOWN B has a mess in his hands.)*

CLOWN A: **Now we put the banana in the right pocket.** *(He does this; so does CLOWN B, reacting. When both bananas are in their respective pockets, CLOWN A notices CLOWN B.)* **Are you doing The Banana Illusion with me?** *(CLOWN B nods.)* **OK, let's go to the final part. Now we raise our right hands.** *(They do.)* **At the count of three, we will crush the banana from the outside of the pocket.** *(CLOWN B reacts with sad face.)* **One** . . . **two** . . . **three!** *(CLOWN A does it, but CLOWN B just touches his pocket with one finger.)* **No, that's not the way, let's do it again.** *(They do it again, and this time CLOWN B crushes his messy banana and cries. NOTE: The banana is inside the hidden plastic bag.)*

237

What's the matter? *(CLOWN B shows his mess to CLOWN A.)* **Forgive him, Lord, he doesn't know what he's doing.** *(To CLOWN B)* **Why did you use a *real* banana?**

CLOWN B: You said The *Banana* Illusion.

CLOWN A: Yes, but it wasn't a real banana. Did you listen to my instructions?

CLOWN B: No. I was out looking for a banana.

CLOWN A: You know, that's what happens when Christians don't listen to God. When the pastor is preaching and some people are not listening, they miss God's instructions for their lives. Now, I hope you have learned your lesson, and I hope next time you listen first!

CLOWN B: I promise! *(They exit together.)*

Looking for God in
All the Wrong Places
Based on I Kings 19:9-14

by Carolyn Costley
(Spatz & Spatz, Jr.)

(This is the "still small voice" passage. Elijah is upset about all the bad things going on — so many that he can't handle them all by himself anymore. He sure could use some help. So, he goes to a cave to get away and look for God.)

CAST: Three CLOWNS, NARRATOR.

PROPS: A kite, tree branch skewered with giant marshmallows.

(CLOWNS mime the concepts in first paragraph with very little movement. NARRATOR reads slowly, pausing for appropriate action.)

NARRATOR: **God's people are homeless ... They're hungry ... They're polluting the earth ... They don't appreciate the arts ... They don't have any fun ... They're helpless ... They're hopeless ... And they don't go to church!**
   So Elijah looked for God. *(CLOWNS exit, so they can enter one at a time for the next scenes.)*
   Elijah found God in the wind. *(CLOWN enters with kite. CLOWN shouts: NOT!)*
   Elijah found God in the earthquake. *(Next CLOWN enters and "shakes," holding onto everything. Both CLOWNS shout: NOT!)*
   Elijah found God in the fire. *(Last CLOWN enters with "marshmallowed" tree branch. CLOWNS shout: NOT!)*
   Elijah thought God might be lost. *(CLOWNS look under things, around corners.)*
   But he's NOT. *(CLOWNS make eye contact with*

239

congregation. Point or put hand to ear, listening to their "still small voices.") **He's in *your voice.***

NOTE FROM CAROLYN: This skit can be performed by more than three clowns. Three would still exit at paragraph two; the rest would remain On-stage, looking for God. All clowns would shout the "NOTs."

Follow the Yellow Brick Road

by Kay Turner
(Sweet Pea)

CAST: Seven silent CLOWNS.

PROPS: Bible, several sheets of yellow construction paper, seven printed cards with strings to hang around neck — GOSSIP, HATRED, INDIFFERENCE, DISHONESTY, IDOLATRY, ANGER, DOROTHY.

SETTING: Yellow sheets are placed to represent the "yellow brick road." Bible is on stand at end of road.

MIME SKETCH: First six clowns enter, each wearing card around neck to display his or her characteristic. Each "claims" a location along the yellow brick road.

Dorothy enters and travels along the road. She passes each clown, who offers to give her the trouble he/she wears. She does not accept or reject any of them but seems very confused.

At the end of the road, Dorothy finds a Bible and begins reading. The words seem to give her strength. *(Shows muscles in her arm.)* Taking the Bible with her, she now travels back down the road, but this time she has the strength to reject each clown along the way.

Dorothy stops at road's end and shows victory, then begins reading the Bible again. The other clowns show interest, surrounding her. All exit together, reading the Bible.

Wise and Foolish Builders

Based on Matthew 7:24-27

A Balloon Routine
by Tommy Thomson
(Clownbo)

First, build a balloon house — see illustrations on page 243.

Background Music: "The Wise Man Built His House Upon a Rock." (This song may be found in *Psalty's Songs for Li'l Praisers,* copyright © 1991 World Music Co., Waco, TX, as well as many other children's songbooks.)

Clown wears gloves.

As first verse is sung (by back-up group or congregation, or both), clown stretches and squeezes balloon house, but it does not burst. (End of verse is, "But the house on the rock stood firm.")

For second verse, clown has two pins, one concealed in a finger of each glove (which he did not allow to touch balloons during first verse). He bursts the balloons, deflating the house as the words are sung, "The house on the sand fell down."

NOTE FROM TOMMY: It's fairly quick, lasting only as long as the song, but has proven to be a very impressive lesson.

I only use 260A modeling balloons.

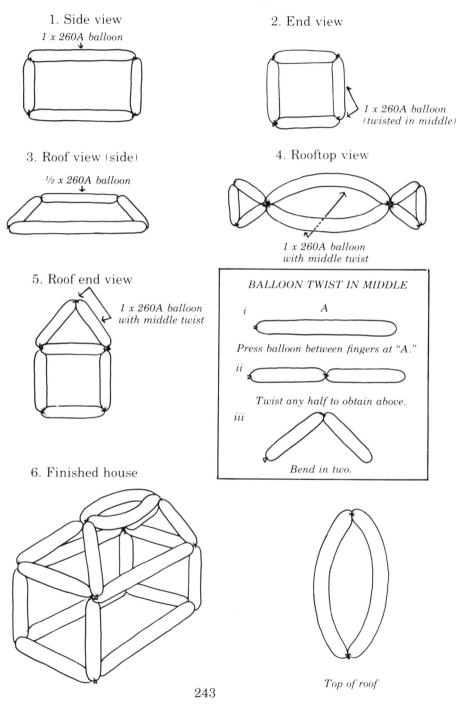

1. Side view

1 x 260A balloon

2. End view

*1 x 260A balloon
(twisted in middle)*

3. Roof view (side)

½ x 260A balloon

4. Rooftop view

*1 x 260A balloon
with middle twist*

5. Roof end view

*1 x 260A balloon
with middle twist*

BALLOON TWIST IN MIDDLE

i   A

Press balloon between fingers at "A."

ii

Twist any half to obtain above.

iii

Bend in two.

6. Finished house

Top of roof

243

No-Prop Clowning

by J. T. Sikes
(Bubba D. Clown)

"Where did I put that rope trick? Where's my puppet? I know I brought those walkaround gags — where are they?"

Whether you call them pocket magic, balloons, stickers, puppets, walkaround gags or giveaway items, they are still props that you depend on. So, here's the big question: *What would you do without your props?*

And here are some answers:

1. Stand in one spot and start looking and pointing into the air. While you are pointing, make sure you change the expression on your face. Show excitement, inquisitiveness, enjoyment and surprise. In no time you will have a large group of people looking into the air, asking one another what you are looking and pointing at. This is fun.

2. Start walking behind someone, fairly close. Mimic the person in front of you. If they turn around, stop quickly and look at something else, as if you were not following. Then when they start off again, quickly follow. Start and stop as often as you need, to get response from the crowd. People always laugh at this one.

3. If you are in front of a store or an entrance to a building, pretend that you are a motorized dummy. Make short choppy motions with your hands and arms and stare off into space. People will come up to you to see if you are real. Continue your motions until a large group comes by, then simply start walking in with them. Make your motions smooth and friendly — you don't want to scare them to death! (In the USA I usually speak softly to them, and that gets a laugh.)

4. This one always takes children by surprise: Stand there, being extra-conservative and proper as long as the parents are looking. As soon as the parents look away, make the craziest face possible at the children. When parents look back,

be prim and proper again. Not only do children love this, so do people watching from the sidelines.

5. Mimicking adolescent boy/girl attraction always goes over big. Go to someone and start pointing to a stranger of the opposite sex. Use quick little motions as if to ask, "Are you two in love?" (Remember, these kids do not know each other.) If they pretend to ignore you, make your motions larger and larger until a crowd is attracted. (Believe it or not, it's usually the boys that turn bright red while their buddies roll on the floor.) You can also stand there pretending to shoot cupid's arrows at them, or exaggerate your beating heart. Don't forget to add plenty of facial expressions. This really draws a big crowd in the malls.

6. Did you know that one of the easiest and most enjoyable things you can do is just walk around and wave to people? Try all the different waves you can think of — the shy wave with your hand covering your face, the rolling finger wave, the arcing wave, etc. People will love you for that simple wave and friendly smile. Be creative, and see just how many different ways you can wave at someone.

7. When someone is walking by, wait until they get real close, then start pointing down at their shoes. As they look down, say to them, "Your feet are moving." If they stop (They usually do), say to them, "Never mind, they've stopped." By this time the person has caught on to the trick; but, always tell them, "They've started to move again," as they walk away.

NOTE FROM J. T.: As you can imagine, there are many other ways to be funny without using props. Today, we live in a world where kids are always expecting something. It's no different when they see a clown. "Give me a sticker, give me a balloon, I want one of those rings." Well, folks, you can give them something. Give them the joy of seeing a clown artist. Give your time, your heart, your love of fellow man, and the countless hours of training and practice it takes to be the best clown you can be. Give them yourself, and ask nothing in return except those priceless, wonderful, radiant smiles on their faces. No-prop clowning? YOU BET! Give it a try, and see if it doesn't make you a better clown.

Things Aren't Always What They Seem

by J. T. Sikes
(Bubba D. Clown)

J. T. SAYS: Today we are faced with an ever-increasing threat to the children of our country. This threat comes in several forms, including drugs, alcohol, and child abuse. With this in mind, I developed this little routine that is included in all of my events — my show, birthday parties, and gospel services. It is my belief that as a responsible performer, my civic duty is to teach children about these dangers. This is done with the children's interest at heart, and parents, teachers, and ministers all thank me afterwards. By incorporating this simple routine into your regular show, the children will understand this important message in a way they won't soon forget.

INFORM THE CHILDREN

CAST: SOLO CLOWN.

PROPS: Empty "Pringles" potato chip can with two spring snakes inside.

ROUTINE: **As the show or party progresses, usually about in the middle, I tell the kids, "Wow! This is the part of the show where I take a break. It's kinda like a snack time. Excuse me, gang. It will only take a couple of seconds to grab a little snack. You see, I've gotta keep my energy up for the rest of the show."**

Now I bring out my FAKE CHIP CAN. It looks just like a "Pringles" chip can, and the kids accept it as chips. Just before I open the can I ask, "Would you like me to share my snack with you?" Of course the answer is always . . . YES!

With that loud answer from the kids, I quickly

take the lid off the can, and out jump two six-foot spring snakes. At the same time I scream real loud, "AAAHHHHHH!" Of course this causes everyone in the room to jump, and I pretend to be real frightened for a moment.

After the snakes are in the audience, I look at the kids and snicker, saying, "I'm sorry I did that to you guys."

As I collect the snakes and start stuffing them back into the can, I point to the can and say, "You know, *things aren't always what they seem.* Let's talk about 'drug pushers,' for example . . . They will try to tell you that their little round pills or rocks are the SUPER-DUPER-IST things in the world. They might even tell you that if you take them, you will feel like 'Snow White' or 'Prince Charming.' They'll also tell you that their little rocks will make your troubles go away. *But do you know what really happens if you take this stuff?"*

At this point the snakes are reloaded and ready to spring out once more. "Yep, you guessed it!" I release the snakes again and scream, "AAAHHHHHH!"

"Wow! Boys and girls, drugs can really scare the SNAKES out of you *and mess up your life.*" As I point to the can, again I say to them, "You know, things aren't always what they seem."

God's Gift Shop

by Dennis Clare

CAST: SOLO CLOWN.

MIME SKETCH: Performer mime goes into a gift shop and starts looking around for a gift. It seems the shop is empty. He or she picks up several gifts, accidentally dropping and smashing one. Very quickly picks it up, but suddenly looks upward and discovers that God has been watching. He/she puts broken gift back on shelf.

God directs performer to rack of coats. Performer is invited to choose one. He/she dislikes the one God wants and puts it back on the rack. Chooses one he/she really likes, but God doesn't like this one. Performer pays no attention to God and continues to put the coat on. It is about three sizes too small, and performer struggles to do up the buttons.

Once it is all done up, he/she parades around the shop, but the coat is too restrictive and movement is difficult. Still paying no attention to God, performer goes to walk out of the shop. In reaching for the door handle, the coat rips. He/she then goes back to show God. God instructs performer to take it off and return it to the rack, trying on the first one God suggested. Performer does this and finds it fits perfectly. He/she offers God some money for the coat, but God conveys the coat is free . . . A free gift.

Performer exits shop, thanking God for the gift.

Meat of the Word?

Based on Hebrews 5:12-14 and Psalm 119:11

by David Ebel
(Happy-Go-Litely)

CAST: Two Clowns — HAPPY (Whiteface), P-NUT (Auguste).

PROPS: Huge hamburger (3' x 1' made of foam), Bible.

HAPPY: *(Calls for P-NUT , who is Off-stage.)* **P-Nut!**

P-NUT: *(Still Off-stage)* **What?**

HAPPY: **What are you doing?**

P-NUT: **Eatin'.**

HAPPY: **You come out here, right now!** *(P-NUT appears with huge hamburger in his hands.)* **Where did you get that?**

P-NUT: **McDonald's.**

HAPPY: **Why are you eating now, in church?**

P-NUT: **I was hungry. No, ah . . . remember you told me to "Eat the meat of the Word" and "Hide God's Word in my heart?" Well, look inside.** *(Lifts up edge of bun.)* **See? It's got my Bible in it!**

HAPPY: *(Shocked)* **I think that you are confused.** *(To audience)* **How many of you sometimes get confused while reading God's Word? . . . Ah, many of you. Well, let's see if I can explain. When the Bible says to "Eat the meat of the Word," it doesn't mean in a hamburger bun . . .** *(To P-NUT)* **When you were born, did you go out right away and eat steak?**

P-NUT: **Yup . . . Sure did!**

HAPPY: **No, you didn't!**

P-NUT: **I didn't?**

HAPPY: **No, you didn't! When you were born, you were**

born without teeth and couldn't eat steak!

P-NUT: Sure I did. I just swallowed it whole!

HAPPY: No, sir. You started out as a baby and drank milk.

P-NUT: Oh, milk. I forgot . . . I was hardly there yet!

HAPPY: And then when you grew older, you could eat meat. That's how it is in your spiritual life. When you give your heart to Jesus and ask him to forgive you for your sins — Jesus died for you to forgive you of your sins — the Bible says you are "born again" of his spirit. The only way to God is to be "born again through Jesus." That means that you are a brand new baby Christian. And baby Christians must begin to understand God's will by drinking the milk of the Word till they grow up. Then they can "eat the meat of the Word." When you grow up, you learn the will of God from prayer, Bible reading, and serving him. That's the meat of his Word!

P-NUT: Oh, I get it . . . But I guess I'll still eat this one. *(Points to big burger.)*

HAPPY: I guess. I'll see you later, if you *ever* finish. Oh, by the way . . .

P-NUT: What?

HAPPY: You said that you got that burger at McDonald's. I've never seen anything like *that* on the menu. What did you ask for?

P-NUT: A quarter ton-er!

HAPPY: Oh, get out of here! *(Chases P-NUT off the stage.)*

The Disappearing Varnish

by Philip Noble
(Rainbow)

(This is a variation on "God Is . . .," page 227.)

CAST: Seven CLOWNS, each carrying a letter card — A, H, I, N, R, S, V; Clown CONDUCTOR.

(CLOWNS enter and try arranging themselves into words, but only get nonsense. CONDUCTOR enters and arranges CLOWNS in a line to spell VARNISH.)

CONDUCTOR: **Ladies and gentlemen, paint is often difficult to remove, but . . . I am now . . . before your very eyes . . . going to make VARNISH disappear.** *(Approaches CLOWN with letter R and directs him to leave stage. He then pushes other CLOWNS together to read:)*

CONDUCTOR: **However, sin is not so easy to remove, as it is often concealed.** *(All CLOWNS in unison put their letters behind their backs. CONDUCTOR instructs line to turn as one [a "marching" move]. The line now reads:)*

(CLOWNS with H, A, and V move away, leaving SIN.)

CONDUCTOR: **But here is someone who can tell you how to do this for yourself.** *(Introduces the preacher/speaker.)*

Faith — A Gift of God

Based on Ephesians 2:8-9

by Philip Noble
(Rainbow)

CAST: Three CLOWNS, PASTOR/LEADER.

PROPS: Equipment to blow soap bubbles, case containing fishing net, rope, rubber worm, a glass bubble.

MIME SKETCH: Two clowns enter, blowing bubbles all over stage.

Third clown enters with case. He/she sees the bubbles, then tries to catch one. It bursts. He tries again very carefully. Again, it bursts.

Clown 3 opens case, takes out net, and with great energy sweeps up all the bubbles he/she can see. He then looks into the net to lift out the bubbles. Nothing there.

Clown 3 takes piece of rope, ties it to handle of net and fixes a "worm" to the hanging end to go fishing for the bubbles. *(If the worm is soaked in soap solution, it will be almost possible to catch the bubbles.)* But again, Clown 3 fails.

The bubble-blowing Clowns 1 and 2 retreat, leaving Clown 3 with empty case sitting sadly, cross-legged, Center Stage, with net resting over his/her shoulder.

Quietly, the Pastor/Leader comes up behind Clown 3 and slips the glass bubble into net, unseen by Clown.

PASTOR: *(Reading with music or simply speaking)* **"For it is by grace you have been saved, through faith —**

**and this not from yourselves, it is the gift of God —
not by works, so that no one can boast."** (Ephesians
2:8-9, NIV)

(CLOWN 3 slowly discovers the "bubble" and exits.)

Peer Pressure

Based on Acts 4:19

by Mark Seckel
(Marko)

CAST: One CLOWN, parent or fireman to help.

PROPS: A bang wand (see Preparation), small sign — "Do Not Pull."

PREPARATION: The "bang wand" is made with a tube party popper and a long string. Load the tube with party popper and extend string through other side. Color the wand black with white tips. Attach sign to bottom of string. When string is pulled, party popper will "explode" and small streamers will fly out. Party poppers are available at party stores.

CLOWN: How would you like to see a new trick I've been learning? *(Kids always say yes. CLOWN plays with them, gets them excited about seeing new trick. Then he pulls out the bang wand and holds it up high.)* **Good, I brought it with me today just for you!**

(Notices the string and points to it.) **Hey, what's this?** *(While pointing to string, follows it down to sign and reads aloud.)* **Do Not Pull. Hey, folks, should I pull this?** *(Plays with kids, getting them to tell him to pull it. However, he acts as if it is against his better judgment to do so.)* **Well ... if you insist.** *(Pulls the string and party popper goes off.)*

(Parent or fireman enters and asks if anyone heard a noise. He/she notices the bang wand and says, "Hey, the string is gone! Did someone pull it?" Kids always tell on the CLOWN. CLOWN and parent/fireman play this up big. Parent/fireman then says that he put the sign on the wand because it is a fire hazard and he didn't want any kids to get hurt. He then leaves stage, saying to CLOWN, "I want to talk to you after the show!")

CLOWN: Ha, ha, very funny. Who told me to pull that string? *(Kids will say they did it.)* **But who got in trouble for it?** *(They will say that you did.)* **Well, kids, I want you to learn from my mistake. The next time your friends want you to do something that you think is wrong, don't do it, because *you* will get in trouble for it . . . and then your friends will laugh at you.**

NOTE FROM MARK: The minute someone says "peer pressure," kids block out whatever comes next. However, by demonstrating it, they get the point and don't realize they've just had a lesson on peer pressure. Also, some church groups are touchy about the phrases magic trick and magic wand. To avoid offense, use the words illusion or illustration instead.

A Little Sin
Is Too Much

by Mark Seckel
(Marko)

CAST: One CLOWN.

PROPS: Electric mixer, dummy electric cord and switch, bottle of soap solution, tarp, sticker with "SIN" printed on it.

PREPARATION: See instructions in Mark's own words on skit development, page 44.

CLOWN: **Hi, kids! Guess what? I have invented something brand new, and something so fantastic that you just won't believe it. Would you like to see what it is?** *(Plays this up to get children involved.)* **Here it is! Marko's new heavy-duty, scrubbly-bubbly, quick and easy — Super Soap! That's right! This new soap is so powerful that you only need one drop to make lots of bubbles. Would you like to see it?** *(Plays up children's reactions.)* **Great! Watch this.**

(Walks over to mixer and stands behind it.) **With only one drop, I will make a lot of soap bubbles.** *(Puts one drop into solution in mixing bowl.)* **Now watch this . . .** *(The children will expect to see lots of soap bubbles, but they won't be prepared for what happens next. CLOWN turns on mixer and waits until bubbles start over the top.)* **How about that?! It works! Look at those bubbles! I'll just turn this off and . . .**

(At this point he tries to turn off the dummy switch. Uses clown skills to get the audience to react.) **Oh, no! Help!!** *(Now he gets the idea to pull cord from mixer — the dummy cord — and communicates this with audience. He has tried using the switch and even pulled power cord from mixer. Still, it just keeps mixing away, making bubbles*

that overflow the bowl. NOTE: In the current version of this skit, Mark uses a clear tube to keep feeding water and soap solution to the mixer bowl. Yes, you will have soap suds everywhere! So protect the floor with a tarp.)

(After CLOWN has done everything he can think of to turn mixer off, he unplugs the real power cord, without letting the audience see. It now seems as though the mixer had a mind of its own and decided to turn itself off. He wonders — why did the experiment work so well? ... Turns to the bottle of solution.) **Oh, no! No wonder it didn't work!** *(Turns bottle around. There is a sticker on it that reads SIN.)* **... This wasn't my bubble solution, this was sin! ... What do you know ... it looks like a little bit was too much!**

(NOTE: Now you can do some teaching on "A Little Sin Is Too Much," but stay in character.)

The Dancing Clown

by Olive Drane
(Valentine)

OLIVE'S BACKGROUND NOTES: Dance is one of the other visual arts that I have explored in the context of worship in church. It seemed natural for me to bring clowning and dance together. The first time I did this was in 1989 for the official opening ceremony of the 2nd Christian Resources Exhibition in Glasgow, Scotland, and then again in the celebration of worship that concluded the same three-day event.

THE DANCE: **The music was Graham Kendrick's song, "Shine, Jesus, Shine," which is very popular in churches throughout the United Kingdom.** *(It is available on a cassette titled* Live Worship With Morris Chapman, *copyright © 1990, Marantha Music, P.O. Box 31050, Laguna Hills, CA 92654-1050. It has also been recorded by many other artists.)* **A group of dancers wore brightly colored dresses and danced the whole song interpretively. The clown came wandering in and was so evidently attracted by the music and color that she tried desperately to join in. But she was unable quite to master it, until the third verse, beginning with the lyrics, "Lord, I come to your awesome presence . . ." In the course of this verse, the clown knelt at the feet of one dancer who stood in the shape of the cross, and then rose to dance the final chorus in unison with the dancers, in a testimony of Resurrection power, as she is transformed into a perfect dancer. It was only afterwards, when I saw a photo of this event, that I realized a large cross had been projected onto the back wall as we danced, dominating the entire scene.**

THE RESULTS: A young female social worker came to

me afterwards, very moved, and said, "That was me kneeling at that cross." And an Episcopalian priest who was also there said to me, "I think when you clown it's like pulling back the curtain and making a space for God to step in."

Rocky the Rock

by Roly Bain
(Roly)

CAST: One CLOWN.

PROPS: Rola-bola (a board balanced on a rolling cylinder), fishing net, crash helmet. A balancing ball may be used in place of the rola-bola.

CLOWN: *(Enters in crash helmet, carrying rola-bola and* fishing net.) **Ladies and gentlemen, boys and girls, a demonstration of ex-traordinary balance and**  **agility coming right up! I thank you** ... *(He fails miserably to stay on the rola-bola, pratfalls, etc. Gets back on.)*

I'm terribly sorry about this. Perhaps I should introduce myself. My name's Rocky — well, it's Simon, really, but everyone calls me Rocky. I used to be a fisherman. Times were hard but good. But then along came Jesus and he invited me to be a fisher of men. Well, I ask you — you can't fit many in *this* net! Still, I gave it a whirl.

I never quite seem to get it right, that's the trouble. I'm always in the right place at the right time, but it always seems to go wrong. For instance, I was up the mountain with Jesus when all of a sudden, Moses and Elijah appeared. It was wonder-ful — one of those moments you want to go on forever. I offered to build them each a chalet right there and then. *(Falls off rola-bola.)* **I shouldn't have.** *(Gets back on rola-bola.)* **... And then there was the time I saw Jesus walking towards us on the water — well, I climbed overboard and started walking to him. Don't know why. I could have waited, and he'd have reached the boat. Anyway, I was going great**

guns till I remembered I couldn't swim! *(Falls off; gets back on.)* ... Another time was when we were coming into Jerusalem. It was all going great, the crowds were cheering. I'd sworn I'd never desert him ... and within a few hours I denied him three times. *(Falls off; gets back on.)* The man that I loved, whom I'd followed, given up everything for — I denied him three times. Even after he rose from the dead! Funny, how we say that so matter-of-fact now, but I suppose it is a matter of fact! ... It was the first time I'd seen him. He offered me some fish for breakfast, there by the lakeside, and I could have sworn he asked, "Do you love cod?" I said I liked tuna and haddock, and even a bit of swordfish, but yes, I loved cod. "Me, you fool." *(Falls, get back on.)* "Do you love me?" he said.

One day I got it right! He was asking us who we thought he was, and I knew. From somewhere, somehow, I knew. And I said, "You are the Christ, the Son of the living God." (Matthew 16:16, NIV) **And in that moment I wasn't rocky at all, I could stay on this thing!** *(Stays solid on rola-bola. In all other examples, he's fallen off at the appropriate moment.)* "You're not Rocky," said Jesus. "You're the Rock, and on this rock I will build my church." Wow! I thought, I'm going to be the Rock ... *(Falls off spectacularly; gets back on.)*

But that's always the way. What I've discovered is that if I let the Spirit fill me, I have the power, the vision, the words to do anything. All things are possible. But if I try to do it on my own, I can do nothing, nothing at all.

I'm still Rocky, still the same foolish guy, but God wants me, just as he wants you, however rocky you are, because he builds his churches and his

Church, this church, on rocky rocks — improbable people in impossible places.

And he gives us the keys of the kingdom . . . It beats fishing!

BIBLIOGRAPHY

Encyclopedia Americana. New York: Rand McNally & Company, 1963.

Myers, Robert J. *Celebrations: The Complete Book of American Holidays.* Garden City, NY: Doubleday & Company, Inc., 1972.

Sarnoff, Jane and Reynold Ruffins. *Light the Candles! Beat the Drums!* New York: Charles Scribner's Sons, 1979.

ALPHABETICAL INDEX
OF SKITS BY TITLE

265

ABOUT THE AUTHOR

Photo by Dickinson-Brouwer Photography

Janet Litherland is the author of the best-selling *The Clown Ministry Handbook,* the first complete text on the subject.

She is also the author of several works reflecting the arts in ministry, including plays, monologs, mime skits, Readers Theatre scripts, and liturgical dance choreography.

Besides *The Clown Ministry Handbook,* her other books include *Storytelling From the Bible, Getting Started in Drama Ministry, The Complete Banner Handbook,* and *Absolutely Unforgettable Parties!*

In addition to her freelance writing career, Janet works as an editorial associate for a Florida magazine. She and her husband, Jerry, have two grown sons.

ORDER FORM

MERIWETHER PUBLISHING LTD.
P.O. BOX 7710
COLORADO SPRINGS, CO 80933
TELEPHONE: (719) 594-4422

Please send me the following books:

_____**Everything New and Who's Who in**
Clown Ministry#CC-B126   **$10.95**
by Janet Litherland
Profiles of clown ministers plus 75 skits for special days

_____**The Clown Ministry Handbook #CC-B163**   **$9.95**
by Janet Litherland
The first and most complete text on the art of clown ministry

_____**Storytelling From the Bible #CC-B145**   **$9.95**
by Janet Litherland
The art of biblical storytelling

_____**Getting Started in Drama Ministry #CC-B154**   **$9.95**
by Janet Litherland
A complete guide to Christian drama

_____**Get a Grip! #CC-B128**   **$9.95**
by L. G. Enscoe and Annie Enscoe
Contemporary scenes and monologs for Christian teens

_____**Sermons Alive! #CC-B132**   **$12.95**
by Paul Neale Lessard
52 dramatic sketches for worship services

**These and other fine Meriwether Publishing books are available in
your local Christian bookstore or direct from the publisher. Use the
handy order form on this page.**

*I understand that I may return any book
for a full refund if not satisfied.*

NAME: _____

ORGANIZATION NAME: _____

ADDRESS: _____

CITY: _____ STATE: _____ ZIP: _____

PHONE: _____

☐ **Check Enclosed**
☐ **Visa or Mastercard #** _____

Signature: _____   *Expiration*
                                                  Date: _____

(required for Visa/Mastercard orders)

COLORADO RESIDENTS: Please add 3% sales tax.
SHIPPING: Include $1.50 for the first book and 50¢ for each additional book ordered.

☐ *Please send me a copy of your complete catalog of books and plays.*